THE NEW METHOD TO ACHIEVE
OPTIMUM MUSCULARITY

PRECISION TRAINING

JOHN LITTLE AND PETER SISCO
CREATORS OF POWER FACTOR TRAINING

POWER FACTOR PUBLISHING ■ BOISE, IDAHO

PRECISION TRAINING:
The New Method to Achieve Optimum Muscularity
© 1995 by Power Factor Publishing

Power Factor Publishing Inc.
10400 Overland Road, Suite 383 ■ Boise, Idaho 83709
ISBN #1-886691-18-5

Photography by Mitsuro Okabe
Book design by Dunn+Associates, Hayward, WI
and Sara Patton, Maui, HI

CONTENTS

Section One
THE FUNDAMENTALS

Section Two
ADVANCED PRECISION TRAINING

Contents

PREFACE

In 1993 we introduced a totally new methodology of strength training to the bodybuilding community through a training manual entitled *Power Factor Training — The Science of Bodybuilding.* We expected a modest interest from the relatively small community of bodybuilding enthusiasts. What we received was an overwhelming response from bodybuilders around the world, accolades from the medical and academic communities, exposure in every major bodybuilding publication, requests for seminars, and thousands of phone calls and letters from bodybuilders and athletes who were improving their physiques to unprecedented levels. Moreover, these improvements were being made with fewer workouts than these athletes had been doing in the past. Power Factor Training went through four printings in twenty-two months.

As word of mouth spread to athletes in other sports, and to regular folks who just wanted to be in better shape, we received more and more requests for a book that would adapt Power Factor Training principles to people who wanted the benefits of more muscularity but did not want to take up bodybuilding as a full-time hobby — people who wanted optimum results in minimum time. The training manual you hold in your hands is the response to those requests.

Precision Training is designed to permit you to achieve your optimum muscularity with the greatest efficiency possible. What you consider to be optimum muscularity will vary depending on your reasons for wanting greater strength. A person who wants to burn more calories while at rest needs only a little more muscularity; whereas a tennis player, for example, will want a little more muscle, and a football player will want all the muscle he can achieve. Each can achieve his or her desired optimum level of muscularity faster than previously thought possible, and maintain it with fewer workouts than ever thought possible, using the efficiencies inherent in Precision Training.

— PETER SISCO

INTRODUCTION

We are aware that the whole concept of "strength training" has a negative connotation for many. Images of massive brutes, with Cro-Magnon intellects, who have nothing better to do with their time than try to lift a few more pounds. Fortunately, strength training, qua strength training, is completely divorced from this picture. Strength training is simply that: training for strength. You are training to increase your present strength levels and with it your lean body mass. When you are stronger, day-to-day activities that would normally be considered a bother or a labor are no longer considered problematic — because they're not. You are able to do more things with less effort when you're stronger.

Strength training, you'll be pleased to note, needs to be performed — at the most — three times per week. In fact, we've recently discovered that, once you reach the advanced levels of Precision Training, you'll need to be training only once a week — and probably even less. We are aware that this sounds too good to be true. However, as you'll learn, the facts suggest a very real relationship between work output and recovery ability and, the stronger one becomes (i.e., the greater the work output), the longer it takes his or her body and recuperative subsystems to recover from each workout.

Still, some trainees are a little intimidated by the thought of going to a "hard-core gym" and having some Herculoid in a tank top (usually plastered to his body like the label on a champagne bottle) bark out commands and exhortations such as "No pain, no gain!" at them for hours on end. Who wouldn't be? The truth of the matter is, however, that you don't need (a) the Herculoid, (b) the hard-core gym, or (c) the exhortations.

All you need to make dramatic gains in muscle mass are three things: (1) the right equipment, which, at a brass tacks beginner's level, is simply barbells, a bench, a logbook, and a stopwatch, (2) the motivation to improve your existing physical condition, and (3) the knowledge of how to do so. *The manual you are now holding in your hands contains all the knowledge you'll need to completely tune up and shape up your body to the optimum level of muscularity you choose.*

The Precision Training System is based on the immutable laws of physics and physiology as applied to the realm of strength training and lean body mass development. As of this writing, the success rate of those who have employed our methods has been nothing short of astounding. According to exercise science professionals such as Dr. James Wright, Ph.D., our approach has, quite literally, revolutionized the bodybuilding industry.

Our training system was initially called "Power Factor Training," by virtue of the fact that one of its chief components is a "Power Factor": a measurement of your rate of muscular output. However, after nearly two years of training individuals, quantifying their results in 58 countries, and conducting scores of seminars, interviews, and consultations in which we've fielded questions on all aspects of the system, and by seeing the tremendous results firsthand, we realized that what we were offering people was a precise method of training which, according to exercise physiologists, medical doctors, and chiropractors, was something new, revolutionary, and long overdue.

As you will discover when reading these pages, this is something exciting, different, and, most importantly, productive. The guesswork has finally been taken out of getting into the best shape you've ever been in.

— JOHN LITTLE

DEFINITIONS

"First, let us define our terms."

— SOCRATES

Sets, Reps, and Power Factors (the jargon of Precision Training). Individuals who engage in bodybuilding are a genuine subculture of the population. Consequently, there exists among the practitioners of this sport a jargon that, to outsiders, sounds as foreign as Caesar's Latin. Terms such as reps, bi's, tri's, supersets, pre-exhaustion, forced reps and negatives are common terms to the bodybuilder but leave the initiate looking like a deer caught in the headlights of an oncoming car.

The terms of the bodybuilder, fortunately, are not as intimidating as they may at first appear. Further, it's not even necessary for the average athlete to learn more than a quarter of them. As many terms relate to more advanced techniques of training (designed to add muscle mass to the more seasoned physique — see Section Two: Advance Precision Training), they are not necessary for the purposes of 99% of trainees. We will concentrate on the few that you will need to know in order to understand Precision Training.

Reps: The contraction and/or extension of a muscle group from a starting position of full extension to a finish position of full contraction and its subsequent return to the starting position is called a repetition or "rep." A series of such movements are, naturally enough, described as repetitions.

Sets: A collection of repetitions (anywhere from 1 to 100 or more). Generally, a brief rest of between 30 to 90 seconds is taken after performing a series of repetitions in order to allow the trainee to catch his breath and provide time for the muscle group involved in the set to partially recuperate.

Poundage: The amount of weight or resistance that you will be using on your exercises.

One Rep Maximum: The heaviest amount of resistance that you can lift for one repetition.

Routine: The sum total of reps, sets and exercises in any given workout or training session.

Overload (Muscular Overload): The total amount of work performed by the muscles while lifting weights.

Progressive Overload: An increasing progression, from workout to workout, of the total amount of work performed by the muscles while lifting weights. Only when the overload reaches an amount greater than what the muscles are normally used to performing does an adaptive response (i.e. growth) take place.

Power Factor (PF): The Power Factor is a measurement of the intensity of muscular overload during an exercise. It is measured in pounds per minute. (i.e. $PF = W \div t$ where, PF is the Power Factor, W is the total weight lifted in pounds and t is the total time in minutes)

Power Index (P_i): The Power Index is a measurement of the duration of a given Power Factor. (i.e. $P_i = W^2 \div t \times 10^{-6}$ or $PF \times W \div 1,000,000$ where, P_i is the Power Index, W is the total weight lifted, t is the total time in minutes and PF is the Power Factor) The Power Index is measured on a logarithmic scale and is intended as a relative indicator of muscular output. There are no units of measurment. The Power Factor and Power Index measurements are innovations of Peter N. Sisco.

Productive Workout: A workout of sufficient over-load to trigger a growth response in the Central Nervous System causing an increase in muscle size and strength.

A Brief Lesson in Anatomy & Physiology: Before you can effectively train your muscles, you need to know how they function in order to select the exercises best suited to stimulate them to grow. Without making this a complicated Physiological dissertation, let's examine just a few of our bodies' basic structures and see how they work together and, how this knowledge will make you a more successful in your quest to build a stronger and better-looking body.

Central Nervous System: The Central Nervous System (or C.N.S.) is of vital importance to both the aspiring and competitive bodybuilder as, without nerves, we'd be immobilized because our muscles wouldn't contract. The Central Nervous System itself consists of the spinal cord and brain and functions in conjunction with the peripheral nervous system which is comprised of the ganglia and nerves that reside outside of the brain and spinal cord. The nervous system appears like thousands of little wires that function as transmitters, receivers and interpreters of data from all parts of the body. The nervous system is responsible for stimulating the mus-cles of your body to contract.

Ligaments: Ligaments function to bind bone to bone. They're fibrous bands and their compactness determines to a very large extent the flexibility of the joints they serve. Caution must be exercised when train-ing because, if a ligament is stretched too far, the joint it holds together will become loose, resulting in perma-nent damage of this tissue.

Tendons: Tendons are dense bands at the ends of muscles. Their function is to attach muscle to bone. In the tendons themselves are the Golgi tendon organ, the function of which is to send signals to the brain indicating stress and fatigue levels. Generally, the ache that you experience during strenuous exercise is being transmitted via the tendon and not the muscle.

Bones: There are 206 bones in our bodies that, collectively, comprise our skeleton. Muscles, as we have seen, are attached to bones by tendons and assist us in moving from one position to another.

Muscles: There exist three distinct kinds of muscle tissue within the body; Cardiac, Skeletal and Smooth. Cardiac muscle is in the heart, smooth muscle assists organs such as the stomach and intestines in the passage and digestion of food, while skeletal muscles are responsible for moving our bones. With Precision Training we're looking to increase the size of our skeletal muscles. There are over 600 skeletal muscles in the body, which reveals a ratio of almost three to one of skeletal muscles to bones, and accounts for our highly evolved dexterity and precision in movement.

Muscle Tissue and Overcompensation: Increasing muscle size isn't as complicated as some authors may have led you to believe. The process itself is referred to as hypertrophy and occurs as a direct result of demands placed upon a muscle and the nervous system that is attached to it. The signal for hypertrophy is overload; i.e., making the muscle work harder than it is normally accustomed. In order to overload a muscle you need to apply a load or a resistance for the muscle to contract against and that resistance must be progressive from one workout to the next. That's it. The bottom line in the quest for bigger and stronger muscles is progressive resistance. If you're able to increase your resistance by your next workout, its because your muscles have overcompensated from your previous training session by getting bigger and stronger.

CAUTION

This program involves a systematic progression of muscular overload that involves lifting extremely heavy weights. Because of this, a proper warm-up of muscles, tendons, ligaments, and joints is mandatory at the beginning of every workout.

This is a very intense program that requires both a thorough knowledge of proper exercise form and a basic level of strength fitness. Although exercise is very beneficial, the potential does exist for injury — especially if the trainee is not in good physical condition. *Always consult with your physician before beginning any program of progressive weight training or exercise.* If you feel any strain or pain when you start exercising, stop immediately and consult your physician.

Section One

THE FUNDAMENTALS

1

WHY STRENGTH TRAINING IS IMPORTANT

It's been estimated that more than four hundred muscles are responsible for allowing us to go about our daily activities. It's also common knowledge that if we don't make an effort to keep them strong and balanced in relationship to each other, they'll slowly wither away with the passage of time. It's certainly no secret among exercise physiologists that strength training improves posture, helps prevent back pain, and is the foundation of lifelong physical skill, balance, and coordination. However, new research reveals that strength training — performed properly — can also help prevent osteoporosis, enhance the fat-burning process (resulting in a leaner physique), reduce stress, and even help to stave off components of the aging process.

Strength is also one of the major elements in good athletic performance. The other components of speed, mobility, flexibility, endurance, and coordination correlate with an individual's muscular strength.

LOSING FAT BY LIFTING WEIGHTS

That an individual can actually become leaner by engaging in strength training sounds like a contradiction. After all, strength training just builds big, bulky muscles, right? To get "shapely," people are always better advised to engage in aerobics classes, aren't they? Well, evidently, weight training, for years considered the weak sister of health and fitness exercise, might now usurp the throne. Recent studies have proven that strength training, performed for the express purpose of increasing lean body mass, can be more effective than aerobics in reducing stores of subcutaneous fat, resulting in startling changes in one's appearance. The key to unlocking this new appearance lies in understanding how muscle affects metabolism and why body composition is more important than body weight.

Recent studies have proven that strength training, performed for the express purpose of increasing lean body mass, can be more effective than aerobics in reducing stores of subcutaneous fat.

Muscle tissue, unlike fat cells, is what is termed "active" tissue. In other words, a certain number of calories are required simply to sustain its existence. In fact, for every pound of muscle on your body, between 50 and 100 calories are required daily simply to sustain its cellular activity. Therefore, if you were to add one pound of muscle to your frame, your body's natural metabolism would increase by roughly 75 calories — even while you are completely inactive. That may not sound like much, but, given the fact that there exist 3500 calories in a pound of fat tissue, if you were able to sustain that pound of muscle for an entire year, you would lose about eight pounds of fat from your body. Try to envision eight pounds of butter on top of your kitchen table and you begin to get an idea of just how radical a change in appearance that truly is. However, the converse is also true: that is, if you were to lose a pound of muscle tissue to dieting, you would also have lost a certain degree of energy-burning potential, with the result that a certain percentage of the calories you took in on a daily basis would now end up being stored as fatty tissue — with the net result again being a rather profound change in your appearance, this time for the negative.

Wayne Wescott, an exercise physiologist and strength training consultant to the YMCA of USA, recently conducted a study that revealed strength training to be more effective than aerobics for the purpose of losing body fat. Wescott compared two groups of 36 men and women who had completed an eight-week program. All of them consumed a reduced calorie diet made up of 20% fat, 20% protein, and 60% carbohydrates. In addition, the subjects were required to exercise three times per week for 30 minutes a session. One group combined a 15-minute total body strength training program with 15 minutes of aerobic exercise. The other group did 30 minutes of aerobic activity only.

The results were fascinating. According to Wescott, the aerobic-exercise-only group lost an average of 3.2 pounds of fat — which, on the surface, appears to be pretty impressive for an eight-week time investment.

3

Until you contrast their results with what the strength training/aerobic exercise group accomplished! They lost an average of 10 pounds of fat — almost three times more fat loss! It's significant to note that this group also gained two pounds of muscle per person, compared to a loss of a half a pound of muscle per person among the aerobic-exercise-only group.

Another recently completed study, this one conducted by researchers at Emory University in Atlanta, revealed similar findings. Overweight women who either did 20 minutes of aerobics three times a week, or nothing at all, lost only 72% of fat per pound of weight lost. Mary Ellen Sweeney, M.D., of the Emory Health Enhancement Program, commented that "those who did 20 minutes of circuit strength training three times a week retained more muscle," which parlayed into 85% of every pound they lost being from fat tissue.

Knowing that all of us, from age 20 onward, will naturally lose about a half pound of muscle per year (which results in a reduction of ½% from our resting metabolic rate), and in view of the above research information, an effective strength training program would appear to be the most efficient route to obtaining a lean, muscular body and, perhaps more importantly, maintaining it as we get older.

AMMUNITION IN THE WAR AGAINST OSTEOPOROSIS

Strength training yields another dividend: that of increased bone density. Studies have demonstrated repeatedly that physical activity increases bone mineral content and, more specifically, weight-bearing or resistance exercise has been associated with higher bone density. Sports medicine practitioners have universally concluded that strength training is beneficial in the prevention of osteoporosis, a condition which largely affects post-menopausal women in whom the density of bones decreases over time, leading to fractures.

According to recent studies, osteoporosis currently afflicts some 24 million Americans, and one out of every three women in her sixties is estimated to suffer a fracture in the spine because of it. The treatment of osteoporosis is by no means conclusive, but it's clear that lifestyle factors such as exercise influence the development of bone strength.

An interesting fact regarding the significance of resistance on our bones was brought to light by, of all people, the renowned aerobics guru, Dr. Kenneth Cooper, who recently wrote: "Along with many other exciting revelations from the NASA space program, the effect of weightlessness on bone mass reinforced the belief that exercise is important in the maintenance of bone strength. Using techniques which allowed scientists to measure the bone density of the astronauts of Skylab 4 both before and after space flight, it was discovered that weightlessness caused a marked loss of bone strength. In the absence of the pull of gravity, the bones were no longer required to support the weight of the body. As a

Sports medicine practitioners have universally concluded that strength training is beneficial in the prevention of osteoporosis.

consequence, the bones began to deteriorate rapidly. The calcium that was lost from the bones was eliminated from the body through the kidneys in such large amounts that there was actually concern that the astronauts might develop kidney stones in space! NASA's original plans for providing exercise for astronauts in space had centered around providing aerobic exercise to maintain cardiovascular fitness, which can easily be done in zero gravity. They are now working to devise forms of strength training that can be performed in order to protect the astronauts from muscle and bone deterioration." [1]

THE OVER-40 BENEFIT — THE HGH CONNECTION

If you're impressed by the benefits provided by strength training in the above scenarios, just wait until you read the results of a landmark study carried out in 1990 by Daniel Rudman at the Medical College of Wisconsin in Milwaukee. The results of Rudman's research surprised even the gerontologists, who have been talking about it ever since.

Rudman administered Human Growth Hormone (HGH) injections to twelve hormone-deficient men (aged 61 to 81) for a period of six months. After six months of HGH injections, these men increased their percentage of lean body weight (i.e., muscle mass) by 9% — while simultaneously dropping 14% body fat! The incredible component of this study was the fact that these individuals made this spectacular progress *without exercising*. Not only did these individuals gain muscle mass, some even proclaimed a renewed interest in sex. Most claimed that they had "never felt better." Researchers conducting this experiment later wrote in the *New England Journal of Medicine* that the physiological reversal these individuals displayed was comparable to shedding 10 to 20 years of age.

The results of this study so impressed the National Institute on Aging (NIA) that, two years later, it launched nine studies of its own in the U.S. for the sole purpose of determining if HGH could somehow increase the vitality of individuals heading into their autumn years. Others (younger individuals) who have taken

The physical stress of the intense workouts, if performed regularly, can boost the body's natural production of Human Growth Hormone by as much as 50 percent.

HGH injections have gone on record as saying that they find they can now eat their pizzas and drink their beer with impunity; they're getting leaner and stronger — without exercising more — and they're still dropping body fat.

What is so magical about this HGH? Well, as touched upon, HGH is an acronym for Human Growth Hormone, a naturally occurring substance in the human body. Dr. Mary Lee Vance, an endocrinologist who has conducted a hormone replacement study at the University of Virginia School of Medicine in Charlottesville, recently told *Men's Journal* magazine that "Our bodies make less growth hormone in our fifties, sixties, and seventies than they do in our twenties. A lot less. We know growth hormone helps to burn fat and build muscles, and to improve metabolism." She went on to state that, in small doses, the hormone would prove to be basically safe and even beneficial, but cautioned that the results of the present investigations going on around the country would first have to be analyzed before any conclusive statements regarding the compound could be accurately drawn.

Kinesiologist/writer Terry Todd, in the same issue of *Men's Journal*, went on to state that higher than normal levels of growth hormone may result in what he terms "substantial benefits," including a healthier heart, since HGH lowers cholesterol levels in the blood and may further serve to keep fat from collecting around the abdomen, thereby reducing the risk of heart disease. Todd also pointed out that HGH further serves to build "a stronger immune system, quicker healing response, increased sex drive. But it is growth hormone's ability to build muscle mass and reduce fat that is especially striking. Research reveals that the hormone rewires the body's metabolic engine, causing it to burn fat to meet energy demands while converting the building block proteins to muscle."

Not to rain so early on the HGH parade, but there does exist a darker side to this "wonder drug." The problems associated with HGH injections center around determining just where the fine line exists between "ideal" dosage and overdose. This appears to be a highly individual thing, as too much of this apparently "good" thing can produce the following list of problems: carpal tunnel syndrome, osteoporosis, diabetes, arthritis, and heat intolerance. But let's not throw the baby out with the bath water. The problems, as they exist, result from receiving overdoses of the *synthetic* version of this hormone.

What if we could secrete more of this wonderful hormone naturally? What if we could have the benefits of an increased amount of HGH coursing through our bodies — which would serve to stave off the aging process, burn fat, and build muscle mass — without any of the problems associated from potential overdoses and injections of synthetic compounds? Well, obviously it would be great. And greater still is the fact that we can accomplish this. How? Well, again, according to Todd, "High-intensity exercise, free-weight multijoint training, done two or three times a week, handling loads you can lift only a maximum of 6 repetitions (versus lighter weights lifted 15 times or more) appears to stimulate significant HGH production."

If we consider this point for a moment, heavy over-load training, the kind that would see you unable to squeeze out a seventh full-range repetition, would obviously involve the use of a heavy resistance and, if we may extrapolate, the heavier the resistance and the greater our rate of lifting (or muscular output), the more HGH we should be able to secrete naturally. Todd has also stated that "Machines do not produce the same effects, perhaps because you are not enlisting auxiliary muscles to balance the weight, as you are with free weights." But this would appear to be a debatable point. After all, the auxiliary muscles required to balance a weight would be so small that, even collectively, their involvement wouldn't impact one's rate of lifting all that much. The key here would appear to be one's rate of lifting a heavy resistance — whether that resistance is in the form of an Olympic barbell, a Universal machine, or a bucket of rocks.

It would appear that the rate of work one performs plays a significant role in the stimulation of HGH, since even sprinting (where a great amount of work is performed in a given unit of time) is singled out as another form of exercise that's been shown to increase HGH levels. (Todd recommends that, "If you are in good enough shape, slot in sprint work two times a week, since sprinting increases HGH levels much more than long-distance work.")

According to Dr. Mauro Di Pasquale, who teaches at the University of Toronto, the physical stress of the aforementioned workouts, if performed regularly, can boost the body's natural production of HGH by as much as 50%. Evidently the body increases the production of growth hormone in direct response to the exercise, and as preparation for a similar stress on the body some time in the future.

Precision Training, as you shall learn, provides a method that allows you to perform the greatest amount of work in a unit of time, and a precise means to measure your work output to ensure that you're stimulating natural production of your HGH with every workout.

STRESS RELIEF

Obviously total fitness includes the mind as well as the body, and Precision Training is also useful in this regard a means to relieving mental stress. The late Dr. Hans Selye, a pioneer in stress research, wrote at length about how mental stress, if left unchecked, can quickly lead to physical malfunctions. Selye maintained that everything from heart attacks to alcoholism and obesity can be caused by stress, and that the relief of stress can go a long way toward eliminating such problems.

Exercise can provide immediate relief for tension in specific areas of the body, as well as remove the general feeling of lethargy that can result from daily stress.

It's obvious that skeletal muscle strength is integral to our level of physical fitness, but mental well-being also plays a major role in the total outlook of even the fittest athlete. This is not a novel concept by any means. The mind/body relationship was first presented by the Greeks, and then later by the Romans as the ideal we should strive for, with their concept of *mens sana in corpore sano* (a sound mind in a sound body). Wilhelm Reich later concluded that physical problems such as asthma, rheumatism, hypertension, and ulcers were often the result of chronic mental anxiety. Selye's studies in the 1930s added migraine headaches, obesity, heart attacks, and neck pain to Reich's list of stress-related physical maladies. With overcrowded psychiatrists' offices and more people than ever on "stress medications," there can be little doubt that the stress of life is difficult to handle for many individuals, and that it poses a real problem in their day-to-day existence.

But what exactly is stress? And more importantly, how can we take steps to remove or at least lessen its presence in our lives? According to Selye, stress can be defined as "the nonspecific response of the body to any demand." The body's reaction to this is what Selye

11

called the General Adaptation Syndrome, or GAS, a three-tiered response that begins with an alarm stage, followed by a stage of resistance, and finally a stage of exhaustion. The stress itself can cause internal chemical reactions that include the release of adrenaline, increased heart rate, faster reflex speed, muscle tension, and accelerated thought processes. Selye's research indicates that our bodies react exactly the same way to stress — whether it comes in the form of pleasure, success, failure, or depression. Evidently, both "good" and "bad" life situations cause what the body perceives to be stress, and everyone is under some degree of stress, even when asleep.

In other words, stress is the rate of daily wear and tear on our existence. Its effects, however, depend on how we adapt to it and how we're able to dissipate its accumulation of repressed energy. Our General Adaptation Syndrome is always in operation, often on an emergency basis, but the physical outlets for its dissipation are not built in. And it's becoming clear that these dammed up emotions have to be released on a regular basis if we are to stay mentally healthy.

Exercise is the most productive means of release in this regard. Although most active exercises can reduce tension levels in the body, strength training appears to be unique in that it can be pinpointed to the precise area where the stress is located — for example, in the neck, stomach, shoulders, or back. Exercise can provide immediate relief of tension in these areas, as well as remove the general feeling of lethargy that results from our daily wear-and-tear encounters.

All of these life-enhancing benefits do not have to come slowly. In fact, they can come quite rapidly and consistently if certain kinesiological and physiological principles are acknowledged and specific progress calculations are made. These factors are the cornerstones of Precision Training.

THE BENEFITS

Precision Training was designed to yield a three-fold dividend:

1. To promote the highest possible gains in increasing the body's lean tissue mass, strength, natural Human Growth Hormone secretion, stress relief, and resting metabolic rate.

2. To measure the exact quantity of muscular output performed each workout, to make certain that every workout is productive.

3. To determine and monitor each individual's innate adaptability to exercise, so that his or her progress will be consistent and overtraining is avoided.

The supreme importance of muscular overload in building and reshaping the human body has, as we shall see, been established beyond question — both clinically in the lab, and by individuals in the gym during the past five decades. Various training systems deliver various degrees of overload and, consequently, varying degrees of lean tissue stimulation. Until the arrival of Precision Training, however, no training system has ever existed that integrated a precise method of measuring these various degrees of overload, and their varying effects on the muscle growth process systematically. Precision Training, with its revolutionary innovation of the Power Factor and Power Index, achieves all three of these objectives simultaneously. The results it has produced thus far have been absolutely astounding, even to those who are very experienced in bodybuilding, strength training, and physical fitness.

2

STARTING YOUR PRECISION TRAINING PROGRAM

DON'T BE INTIMIDATED

If you are a relative newcomer to weight training, you might be intimidated by all of the equipment involved, the multitude of free (and usually contradictory) advice that is offered in the gym, and the "hardbody" physiques of many of the denizens of the gym. Well, don't be. The fact is that most people who lift weights learned what they know, or think they know, by going into a gym and blindly operating various pieces of equipment, set at an arbitrary weight, until they felt fatigued.

You see this all the time. A guy saunters over to the dumbbell rack and picks up a weight. It feels a little too heavy so he puts it down and picks up a smaller one (without noting the weight stamped on the side.) Then he performs 10 or 15 reps (without actually counting them), and just as it's getting really difficult he puts the weight down and heads to the water fountain for a drink. He returns to his dumbbell (without noting the length of rest he just took) and does some more uncounted reps. When the boredom starts to get to him he moves on to another piece of equipment. That strategy is nothing to be proud of and nothing for you to feel intimidated by.

Precision Training will teach you to see things differently. You will have a keen awareness and appreciation for the role of muscular overload, and you will recognize that overload consists of not just the weight you lift but also the time it takes you to lift it (including the time spent at the water fountain in between sets). You will use this awareness to identify all of the virtually useless exercises that abound, and you will avoid those exercises. You will also completely avoid the overtraining that accompanies the blind, haphazard approach you see everyone else using.

As a result, you will make steady, consistent progress, and with fewer workouts than you ever thought possible. You won't be intimidated because you will soon discover that there are pieces of equipment that cost thousands of dollars and generate very little muscular overload (i.e., they're a waste of your time), and there are popular exercises that generate very little muscular overload (i.e., they're a waste of your time). And you will be able to prove all of this with a stopwatch and a pencil.

In this manual we use terms like "muscle mass," "hypertrophy" and "size and strength" quite frequently, and you might be inclined to visualize a Mr. Universe with huge, bulging muscles and veins. But the truth is that the bodybuilders you see in the magazines are the top *fraction of 1%* of the genetically gifted and mentally disciplined in that sport, and they have spent years to get where they are. There is no more danger that you will suddenly and unexpectedly turn into a massive bodybuilder than there is that you will start tossing a football around, and suddenly and unexpectedly become a better quarterback than Joe Montana.

Using the knowledge in this training manual you'll be able to achieve any level of muscularity you desire, up to the limits of your own genetics and

Precision Training will permit you to engineer each workout so the overload is progressive and your muscularity will increase to the optimum level that you choose.

mental determination. However, the level of muscularity you chose, your optimum level, will be subjective, and dependent on your priorities. Bowling requires less upper body strength than cycling. Swimming requires less strength than football. But remember this: Even if you just want it to be a little less draining to carry the laundry basket upstairs, your goal is still muscle mass and muscle size — just in much smaller amounts. The mass you need might be a mere two pounds, or it might be a bulging forty pounds, but the technique used to obtain it is absolutely identical for both people: progressive muscular overload.

THE THREE FUNDAMENTALS

Precision Training is based on three fundamental principles of exercise science.

1. Your body will only cause your muscles to grow larger in response to an exercise stimulus that is sufficient to signal your brain (central nervous system) that larger muscles are required for survival.

2. Lifting weights is the best means of creating a great amount of work in a unit of time, to trigger the muscle growth process in the central nervous system.

3. The exercise stimulus must be progressive in nature if muscle growth is to continue.

Let's take a brief look at each of these principles.

1. Your body will only cause your muscles to grow larger in response to an exercise stimulus that is sufficient to signal your brain (central nervous system) that larger muscles are required for survival. The human body is very efficient and does not wish to squander its resources. Consequently, it will develop muscles to a point where you can perform daily tasks adequately, but no *more* than adequately. If you are a computer programmer, your body will not supply you with the muscle strength necessary to be a lumberjack. However, if you begin to perform more work that requires bigger, stronger muscles, your body will adapt to that stress by increasing your muscle mass so you can perform that extra workload adequately. Your body does not want you to become frequently exhausted so, when required, it will protect you by growing stronger.

2. Lifting weights is the best means of creating a great amount of work in a unit of time, to trigger the muscle growth process in the central nervous system. Muscles respond to high-intensity exercise by growing

larger. High-intensity exercise involves performing a great amount of work in a unit of time. For example, compare the thigh muscles of a marathon runner with those of a sprinter. Marathoners run at a sustainable pace, doing a nominal amount of work in a unit of time, and therefore have a nominal amount of muscle in their thighs. Whereas sprinters run at the fastest possible pace for a short period of time, performing a great amount of work in a unit of time. Their thigh muscles are huge, and contain the maximum amount of muscle that their genetics are capable of providing. *For strength training, nothing can generate a greater amount of work in a unit of time than lifting weights.* Using Precision Training, you will measure this work with the Power Factor and Power Index.

3. The exercise stimulus must be progressive in nature if muscle growth is to continue. Since your body will grow only enough to perform tasks adequately, you must keep increasing the muscular overload so that the growth does not stop. For example, if last week you performed a workout with X amount of overload, performing the identical workout this week and next week will not promote additional growth, since your body will only adapt enough to cope with X but no more. (Actually a bit more, but just as a safety margin.) Precision Training will permit you to engineer each workout so that the overload is progressive, and your muscularity will increase to the optimum level that you choose. At that point you only need to maintain the overload to maintain your muscularity. Every step is measured with the Power Factor and Power Index.

You will be pleased to learn that your first few months on the Precision Training System will be among the most encouraging of your fitness efforts. The reason is that at no time are the gains quicker or more enjoyable than during the first six months of training. It is at this stage that individuals (whether young or old, and quite irrespective of their level of athletic experience), first become aware of their bodies and notice profound changes starting to happen.

It is also at this point in their training that most individuals who have not utilized any technology on their workouts (i.e., measured their Power Factor and Power Index) make the tactical error of increasing the volume and/or the frequency of their workouts. The result is that, in a matter of months, what started out as rapid gains will grind to a halt. The reason, in a word, is overtraining. No trainee, no matter what his or her level of development, needs to train more than three days per week — at least if making every workout productive (and not simply visiting the gym) is his goal. As strength increases, most people will get productive results by training as infrequently as once a week or even less.

This chapter, then, serves as both a beginner's guide and an experienced trainee's refresher course on the basic elements of increasing lean body mass.

KNOWING WHERE YOU STAND PHYSIOLOGICALLY

Before starting a new training program, *it is of paramount importance to know your existing physical condition*. In fact, an annual physical examination is recommended for everyone starting a new fitness program, whether or not the program includes strength training. If your personal physician gives you the okay to initiate your program, then — and only then — should you proceed.

The program you're about to embark on will, if followed to the letter, improve your health, strength, and muscle tone to such a degree that both you and your physician should be shocked at the metamorphosis. If you're significantly underweight, be prepared to gain up to 30 pounds of rock hard muscle mass. And if you're overweight with no discernible shape, be prepared to become firm; develop a V-shape; lose inches off your waist; shape and expand your chest, shoulders, and arms; while firming up your glutes, thighs, and hips.

THE NATURE OF ADAPTATION (HYPERTROPHY)

It should be understood that muscle growth is a product of hypertrophy, or the enlarging of existing muscle cells. This was established more than 96 years ago, by the research of Morpurgo, and has been reaffirmed conclusively since.[2] The process of hypertrophy is one of muscular adaptation to imposed overload, and occurs only through an increase in the cross-sectional area of a muscle's fibers. The muscle growth process, then, can be triggered only by overloading a muscle.

Research conducted by Roux-Lange[3] indicated that "Only when a muscle performs with greatest power, i.e., through overcoming a greater resistance than before in a unit of time, will its functional cross-section need to increase. . . . Hypertrophy is seen only in muscles that must perform a great amount of work in a unit of time." Further research by Petow and Siebert[4] put a finer point on the overload issue: "Hypertrophy results from an increase in the *intensity* of work done, whereas the total *amount* of work done is without significance." These results are significant for a number of reasons, particularly for "clean" athletes (non-drug–using trainees), as they were obtained a full 10 years before testosterone was first isolated, which meant that all of the subjects participating in the study were unquestionably "natural." As current drug testing of experimental subjects represents a prohibitive and impractical cost, not all conclusions obtained today from training research can be said to be "apples to apples" in terms of their application to natural bodybuilders.

It logically follows that a training method that provides the greatest overload will stimulate the greatest muscle growth.

Further, the research conclusions just quoted demonstrate clinically that, for clean athletes, the amount of time spent training, as opposed to the intensity of muscular output, was not a contributing factor to the muscle growth process. Research conducted by Dr. Arthur H. Steinhaus[5] indicated that, "Only when intensity is increased [overload] does hypertrophy follow." The implications of such data are certainly startling in light of many of our current training trends. For instance, the belief that natural bodybuilders need periodization (factoring into your workouts periods of lower intensity training) to stimulate muscle growth doesn't ring true according to this research. In fact, these studies prove conclusively that muscle grows larger solely in proportion to the pounds per minute work volume (i.e., overload) applied to them — and nothing else. The greater the intensity or overload, the greater the hypertrophy. Think about this for a moment.

Although we touched on the issue of progressive resistance and overload earlier, it bears pointing out that once overload has been clearly isolated as the sole stimulus that induces muscular hypertrophy, it logically follows that a training method which provides the greatest overload will thereby stimulate the greatest muscle growth. In fact, it was this unambiguous conclusion that led to the development of Precision Training.

THE TRI-PHASE

In order for an increase in muscular mass to occur, three distinct phases must take place. The first phase is that growth must be stimulated within the body, which, as we've learned, can only be accomplished through subjecting your muscles, and more specifically, your nervous system, to a previously unencountered level of overload. This is best done by lifting weights, as opposed to other forms of less strenuous exercise. Weightlifting generates the highest possible muscular overload in the shortest possible time.

The second phase is recovery. Both the body and the systems that feed the body must be given time to replenish their energy reserves after a maximum overload workout. Immediately after a workout this becomes the body's first priority. The first order of business is for your body to return to its normal state by recovering from all of the biological demands of your workout. (If your body never recovered from all the forms of exercise you perform in a day you would soon be dead.)

The third phase is the growth process itself, which can take place only after the recovery process has run its course. Recent studies have indicated that the actual growth process may be as little as 15 minutes, and it may occur while you sleep. It is this growth process that allows you to return to the gym and perform a workout at yet a higher rate of muscular overload. And while the overload will actually be higher, the workout will not be perceived as more difficult, because of the fact that you now possess more strength. This is the keystone of "progressive overload" training.

LOCALIZED MUSCLE RECOVERY VERSUS SYSTEMIC RECOVERY

With Precision Training it's been established that, for the purpose of building muscular mass, working out any more than three days per week is a mistake. This does not refer simply to localized muscle recovery, but rather to the recovery of the physical system as a whole. Localized muscular recovery actually takes place very rapidly (24 hours in some cases). However, if you perform 10 sets of heavy squats on Monday, your legs may well have recovered by Tuesday, but try to do a heavy back workout. You won't feel the inclination. The reason is simply that your whole system is called upon whenever you exercise. When you trained your legs the day before, demands were made upon all of your body's recuperative subsystems, not just your legs. And since your whole system is called upon to varying degrees, you've got to allow your whole system time to recover after every workout — not just the specific body part that you trained.

HOW MUSCLE FIBERS WORK

In order to understand the logic of Precision Training, you need to know something about how muscle fibers work. Basically, a muscle consists of millions of tiny muscle fibers that perform only one function: they contract, or shorten, when they receive a signal to do so from the brain. For example, to bend your elbow so you can scratch your ear, your bicep muscle contracts, pulling your forearm upward. Logically, there are two methods that your body could use to create the required contraction. Assuming that scratching your ear requires 1% of your bicep's strength, your brain could signal 100% of the muscle fibers to contract by 1%, creating the required force. Or, your brain could signal 1% of the muscle fibers to contract 100%, also creating the required force. (The mathematicians among you will note that there are actually an infinite number of combinations; e.g., 40% of the fibers activated at 2.5% each.) The human body utilizes the latter technique: the all-or-nothing principle of contracting an individual muscle fiber 100% or not at all. This is known as the law of muscle fiber recruitment.

If you need to lift a heavier weight, your brain activates more muscle fibers. Specifically, if you need to lift more weight per unit of time, operating at a higher intensity, your brain will recruit more muscle fibers to create the required force. More force equals more muscle fibers.

Remember that muscle fibers have to be stimulated in order to grow larger. They are stimulated by being used; they are used by being required to create force. Therefore, if you want to create bigger, stronger muscles as quickly and efficiently as possible, you need to use as many muscle fibers as possible in your exercises. In a word, you need to generate the highest "Power Factor" of which you are capable.

3

THE POWER FACTOR AND WHY YOU NEED IT

WHAT IS A POWER FACTOR?

Until now your only means of gauging the value of your workouts has been by feel alone. All other factors being equal (i.e., prior rest, adequate nutrition, etc.), if you felt particularly tired at the end of a workout, you probably assumed it was more productive than your previous one. The truth is, however, that your muscular overload may have been much less than you perceived it to be, owing to inadequate sleep the night before, having consumed the wrong foods, or some other factor. The fact that you ended up tired and sore was not necessarily because you subjected your muscles to a greater overload. In fact, your workout might have been a total waste of time and effort.

As discussed in the last chapter, the keys to stimulating muscle growth are (1) triggering growth by subjecting your muscles to an overload of a great amount of work in a unit of time, and (2) making that overload

The Power Factor is a measurement of the total amount of weight you lift divided by the time it takes to lift it. It's measured in pounds per minute.

progressively greater from workout to workout. Now, suppose you bench press 150 pounds 30 times in 2 minutes today. And that's all you can do — you can't complete one more rep. Then you come back to the gym next week and bench press 150 pounds 30 times in 1½ minutes. And that's all you can do — you can't get one more rep. Both days you lifted 150 pounds for 30 repetitions. But guess what? When you do it in 1½ minutes you are stronger.

If you don't believe me, ask Isaac Newton. It's a law of physics: The only way to lift the same amount of weight in a shorter amount of time is with a stronger "engine." If your muscles (the engine) are capable of lifting at a higher rate, they must be stronger. With conventional weight training, however, the time it takes to perform the lifting is completely ignored. In the above example, if you ignored time, you would enter the results of the two workouts in your logbook and promptly get discouraged that you were not making any progress.

THINKING IN POUNDS PER MINUTE

The Power Factor is a measurement of the total amount of weight you lift divided by the time it takes to lift it. It's measured in pounds per minute. Ask the average person in a gym what he or she bench presses, and the reply might be "I can bench 275." Ask a person who uses Precision Training the same question, and the answer might be "I can bench 5,300 pounds per minute." Because of the laws of physics and the law of muscle fiber recruitment, the latter is a much more comprehensive measurement. Once you begin to think in pounds per minute, your training objectives and progress become crystal clear.

Using Precision Training, you will be able to calculate a precise Power Factor and Power Index for each exercise you perform, and for your entire workout. You will also be able to calculate ahead of time what workout you will need to perform next time in order to meet your goals of increased size and strength. This means that every workout can pay off in gains and, if it doesn't, you'll know exactly why and where you fell short.

You may, for example, find that your shrug power went down 7%, even when your bench press power went up 34% and your overall Power Index went up 25%. This level of precision and isolation represents a revolution in strength training.

WHAT ABOUT DISTANCE?

At this point you might be wondering why we haven't included the distance that the weight travels as part of the power calculation. There are two reasons that it is left out. First, as a practical matter it is difficult to precisely measure the travel of the bar when lifting, especially in movements that involve an arc of motion which require computations using pi (3.14159). Second, the length of your arms and legs isn't going to change over time, so all those distance measurements would just factor out of any comparisons that are made, leaving only differences in the weight lifted and the time. This is why we did not use horsepower or watts to measure the power that your muscles generate. Our Power Factor system of measurement is ideal because of its simplicity and ease of use.

DETERMINING YOUR POWER FACTOR

The purpose of calculating a Power Factor for each exercise that you perform is to provide a precise numerical measurement of your muscular output. Once you have a numerical representation of your output, you can compare the overload and effectiveness of every workout you perform.

For example, examine the two workouts outlined on the next page. These two workouts are very similar, and when you examine them it looks like #2 is the better one because it involves using heavier weight in every exercise. So it would stimulate more growth, right?

Wrong. Actually, Workout #1 has a Power Factor that is 38% higher than Workout #2, and involves lifting an additional 10,135 pounds of weight. Workout #1 represents more work in a unit of time — the key to muscle growth stimulation. It is virtually impossible to precisely gauge that difference by "feel" alone. With Precision Training, measuring by feel is obsolete.

■ WORKOUT # 1

Exercise	Sets	Reps	Weight
Shoulder Press	2	20	150 lbs
	2	20	180 lbs
	3	15	225 lbs
	Time to Complete: 10 minutes		
Lat Pulldowns	2	30	80 lbs
	2	20	90 lbs
	2	15	100 lbs
	Time to Complete: 11 minutes		
Barbell Deadlifts	2	30	135 lbs
	2	20	155 lbs
	2	15	175 lbs
	Time to Complete: 14 minutes		
Total Time to Complete: 41 minutes			

■ WORKOUT # 2

Exercise	Sets	Reps	Weight
Shoulder Press	2	20	150 lbs
	2	12	190 lbs
	2	10	245 lbs
	1	3	260 lbs
	Time to Complete: 13 minutes		
Lat Pulldowns	2	20	90 lbs
	2	15	100 lbs
	2	10	120 lbs
	Time to Complete: 13 minutes		
Barbell Deadlift	2	20	155 lbs
	2	20	175 lbs
	2	15	190 lbs
	Time to Complete: 14 minutes		
Total Time to Complete: 46 minutes			

ANALYZING WITH THE POWER FACTOR

Let's use the Power Factor measurement to examine your shoulder press performance in the example workouts detailed below. In Workout #1 you began by lifting 150 pounds 20 times, and performed two sets, for a total weight lifted of 6,000 pounds Then you performed two sets of 20 repetitions with 180 pounds, which added 7,200 pounds to the total. Finally, you increased the weight on the bar to 225 pounds and performed three sets of 15 reps, to add an additional 10,125 pounds. This brings the total amount of weight you lifted to 23,325 pounds. Since it took you 10 minutes to lift all that weight, your rate of muscular output, or

■ WORKOUT # 1

Exercise	Total Weight	Time	Power Factor
Shoulder Press	23,325 lbs	10 min	2,333 lbs/min
Lat Pulldowns	11,400 lbs	11 min	1,036 lbs/min
Barbell Deadlifts	19,550 lbs	14 min	1,396 lbs/min

Total Workout Weight: 54,275 lbs
Total Workout Time: 41 min
Overall Workout Power Factor: 1,324 lbs/min

■ WORKOUT # 2

Exercise	Total Weight	Time	Power Factor
Shoulder Press	16,240 lbs	13 min	1,249 lbs/min
Lat Pulldowns	9,000 lbs	13 min	692 lbs/min
Barbell Deadlifts	18,900 lbs	14 min	1,350 lbs/min

Total Workout Weight: 44,140 lbs
Total Workout Time: 46 min
Overall Workout Power Factor: 960 lbs/min

Power Factor, was 2,333 pounds per minute (23,325 pounds divided by 10 minutes).

In Workout #2 you started out by lifting the same 150 pounds 20 times for two sets, for a total weight of 6,000 pounds Then, believing that simply adding weight alone would increase your muscular output, you increased the weight to 190 pounds and performed two sets of 12 reps, for an additional 4,560 pounds. Pushing your limit further, you increased the weight to 245 pounds and performed two sets of 10 reps, for an additional 4,900 pounds Finally, still feeling strong, you increased the weight to 260 pounds and squeezed out 3 reps, bringing your total shoulder press weight to 16,240 pounds Exactly 7,085 pounds *less* than the same exercise in Workout #1! Further, since it took 13 minutes to complete the shoulder press workout, your Power Factor dropped to a comparatively dismal 1,249. That's 1,084 pounds/minute *less* than Workout #1 — a much lower intensity of lifting.

And remember, after the last rep on each of these shoulder press workouts, you would have been completely tired out. You would not have been able to complete another rep — you would be "pumped." And by every sensory measure you would feel that you had given your best effort to stimulate growth. But the fact is that by using the correct combinations of weight and repetitions, Workout #1 was 38% more effective at generating muscular overload and the growth stimulation that goes along with it.

The same calculations reveal similar results for both of the other exercises, as well as for the overall workout, which, incidentally, includes the time taken between exercises to rest and to set up the equipment. (That's why the individual times do not add up to the total time.)

FINDING YOUR "SWEET SPOT"

By all measures, Workout #1 is superior. The reason is that there is a relationship between the amount of weight you put on the bar and the number of times you can lift it. It's obvious: If the weight is very light, you can do many reps but it takes a long time. If the weight is very heavy, you can only do a few reps, and the lifting will end very quickly.

For example, using the bench press, suppose that you want to determine your muscular output at the two extreme ends of this spectrum. First you select a very light weight, let's say 10 pounds, and you perform sets of 40 reps at a time. After the twenty-fifth set you are completely fatigued and cannot perform another rep. All this takes 45 minutes. So, you lifted 10 pounds a total of 1,000 times, for a total weight of 10,000 pounds. Since it took 45 minutes to lift all that weight, your Power Factor is 222 pounds/minute. That is a low Power Factor; my grandmother could lift more than 222 pounds/minute!

Next, you test the other end of the spectrum by lifting the heaviest weight you possibly can. So you put 300 pounds on the bar and, mustering all the strength you can, you perform one rep. You rest for a few seconds, then try to get another rep, but you just can't. Three hundred pounds is your one rep maximum. This calculation is easy: Three hundred pounds in one minute is a Power Factor of 300 pounds/minute. Also a very low Power Factor — a fraction of what you are capable of generating.

The above example demonstrates a critically important element of strength training. If you lift too light a weight you cannot generate a high Power Factor. At the same time, if you lift too heavy a weight you also cannot generate a high Power Factor. Somewhere in the middle lies your personal "sweet spot," where the perfect combination of weight, reps, and time yields your highest possible Power Factor. Finding that spot is the key to maximally efficient and productive workouts. By the way, it varies considerably between individuals.

Finding your personal "sweet spot" is the key to maximally efficient and productive workouts.

The graphs on pages 36–37 illustrate this point. Subjects A and B each experiment to determine how the weight they are lifting affects the number of reps they can complete in a 2-minute period. As you can see, Subject A generates his highest Power Factor when he has 140 pounds on the bar. At that weight he can get the best ratio of total weight lifted per unit of time. That is his sweet spot. This concept is the most critical element of Precision Training. Subject A can put more weight on the bar, in fact he can lift 300 pounds; but if he does, the total weight he can lift per minute is greatly decreased.

Since human muscles will only grow stronger and larger when they are taxed beyond their normal operating capacity, it is crucial to discover what your operating capacity is in the first place. Subject A can lift 280 pounds 8 times in 2 minutes, and it will take everything he has to perform those reps, but it is nowhere near his muscles' full capacity for lifting. Therefore, while it might generate some adaptive response, it is very inefficient compared to him lifting 140 pounds 63 times in the same 2-minute period. This is a well-settled principle of physics. An engine that lifts 4,410 pounds per

■ SUBJECT A

Weight on Bar	Total Reps	Total Weight (lbs)	Power Factor (lbs/min)
40	120	4800	2400
60	108	6480	3240
80	96	7680	3840
100	84	8400	4200
120	72	8640	4320
140	63	8820	4410
160	54	8640	4320
180	45	8100	4050
200	36	7200	3600
220	29	6380	3190
240	22	5280	2640
260	15	3900	1950
280	8	2240	1120
300	2	600	300

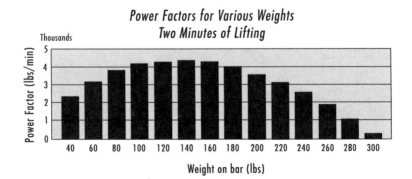

Power Factors for Various Weights
Two Minutes of Lifting

minute has to be more powerful than an engine that lifts 1,120 pounds per minute. Your muscle fibers are the engine; nothing else does the lifting.

Subject B demonstrates how variation occurs between individuals. His highest Power Factor is achieved

■ SUBJECT B

Weight on Bar	Total Reps	Total Weight (lbs)	Power Factor (lbs/min)
40	120	4800	2400
60	111	6660	3330
80	102	8160	4080
100	93	9300	4650
120	84	10080	5040
140	80	11200	5600
160	76	12160	6080
180	72	12960	6480
200	68	13600	6800
220	64	14080	7040
240	50	12000	6000
260	36	9360	4680
280	16	4480	2240
300	4	1200	600

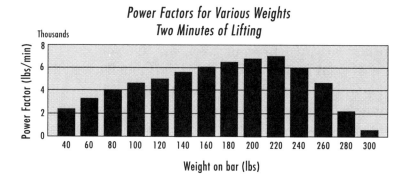

*Power Factors for Various Weights
Two Minutes of Lifting*

when he has 220 pounds on the bar. He can put more or less weight on the bar, but his personal sweet spot is at 220 pounds. Why? There are many factors that contribute to the ability of muscle fibers to activate and to the power they generate. Some of them we know, and some of them we are yet to fully understand. Where the muscle physically attaches to the bone relative to the joint has a profound effect on leverage. The neural pathways between the brain and muscles have varying efficiencies in individuals. The body's ability to supply and process ATP to the muscles varies between individuals, as do the mix of slow-twitch and fast-twitch fibers in each muscle. And the complex cocktail of blood, oxygen, amino acids, and hormones that supply the entire process has nearly infinite possibilities of variation. But here is the good news. All you have to concentrate on is developing your highest possible Power Factor for each exercise, because it gives a clear indication of what is delivering the most overload to your muscles and what is not.

You can't take blood samples and tissue biopsies after each exercise you perform in order to analyze which technique is generating the greatest metabolic changes. You can't place your body in an MRI machine during each exercise to see what area of a muscle is activated by a particular exercise. You can't perform a CAT scan on your brain to determine what neural pathways are being activated by your workout. But you don't need to! If your Power Factor is 6,500 pounds per minute this workout, and last workout it was 5,600 pounds per minute, then you are absolutely, positively generating more output from your muscles. And who cares if it's because of hormone secretion or neural pathways, or both? All these systems work together anyway, so isolating one or the other through complex testing does not really provide any practical benefit to the athlete who just wants results. Train by the numbers and everything else will take care of itself.

SIMPLE ARITHMETIC

As you perform your workout, all you need to do is keep track of how many minutes it takes to

Train by the numbers and everything else will take care of itself.

do each exercise (i.e., bench press, deadlifts, shrugs, etc.), how much weight you're using, and how many reps and sets you do with each weight. Record this information on the Workout Record form.

1. Enter the time of day that you begin your workout. This will be used to calculate your Overall Performance. In all cases you should be sure to warm up fully before starting the clock on your workout. You should first perform your warm-up, taking as long as you like, then start timing your Precision Training. Your warm-up should never be counted as part of your Power Factor. Doing so will lead to an incentive to use heavy weights too quickly, ultimately causing injury. Warm up completely first, then start the clock.

2. Enter the time of day that you finish your workout.

3. Subtract your Start Time from your Finish Time to get the Total Time of your workout. Always express this in minutes only (i.e., 95 minutes, not 1 hour and

WORKOUT RECORD

DATE: 7/16/95 **START TIME:** 8:05 A.M. **FINISH TIME:** 8:51 A.M. **TOTAL TIME:** 46 MIN

■ **EXERCISE:** DEADLIFT

Weight	Reps	Sets	Subtotal
105	× 20	× 2	= 4200 lbs
135	× 20	× 2	= 5400 lbs
155	× 20	× 1	= 3100 lbs
155	× 26	× 1	= 4030 lbs

Exercise 1: Total Weight 16,730 lbs Time 7½ min Power Factor 2231 lbs/min Power Index 37.3

■ **EXERCISE:** BENCH PRESS

Weight	Reps	Sets	Subtotal
120	× 15	× 2	= 3600 lbs
140	× 15	× 2	= 4200 lbs
160	× 13	× 1	= 2080 lbs
175	× 8	× 1	= 1400 lbs
			= 1760 lbs

Exercise 2: Total Weight 13,040 lbs Time 8¼ min Power Factor 1581 lbs/min Power Index 20.6

■ **EXERCISE:** LAT PULLDOWNS

Weight	Reps	Sets	Subtotal
60	× 18	× 2	= 2160 lbs
70	× 18	× 2	= 2520 lbs
80	× 19	× 1	= 1520 lbs
90	× 16	× 1	= 1440 lbs
100	× 13	× 1	= 1300 lbs

Exercise 3: Total Weight 8940 lbs Time 6¾ min Power Factor 1324 lbs/min Power Index 11.8

■ **EXERCISE:** LEG PRESS

Weight	Reps	Sets	Subtotal
300	× 20	× 1	= 6000 lbs
400	× 20	× 2	= 16000 lbs
450	× 20	× 2	= 18000 lbs
500	× 23	× 1	= 11500 lbs
525	× 21	× 1	= 11025 lbs
540	× 19	× 1	= 10260 lbs

Exercise 4: Total Weight 72,785 lbs Time 7⅛ min Power Factor 9705 lbs/min Power Index 706

■ **EXERCISE:** TOE PRESS

Weight	Reps	Sets	Subtotal
350	× 20	× 1	= 7000 lbs
400	× 20	× 2	= 16000 lbs
450	× 20	× 2	= 18000 lbs
500	× 24	× 1	= 12000 lbs
525	× 26	× 1	= 10500 lbs
540	× 17	× 1	= 9180 lbs

Exercise 5: Total Weight 72,680 lbs Time 7 min Power Factor 10383 lbs/min Power Index 755

OVERALL WORKOUT: Total Weight 184,175 lbs Time 46 min Power Factor 4004 lbs/min Power Index 737

Exercise Subtotal = weight × reps × sets ■ Power Factor = lbs/min ■ Power Index = total weight × Power Factor ÷ 1,000,000

© 1995 Power Factor Publishing Inc.

35 minutes). This is entered at the top of the page and at the bottom in the Time section of Overall Workout Performance. The Overal Workout Time includes *all* the time used from the beginning of your workout (not counting the warm-up) to the end. It includes rests between sets, rests between exercises, the time you took changing weights, and the time you took to get a drink of water. It is *not* just the sum of your individual exercise times.

4. The Subtotal weight lifted per set is calculated by simple arithmetic. For example, if you perform 20 repetitions with 105 pounds, you multiply the two numbers to get 2,100 pounds. If you do 2 sets at that weight, you multiply by 2 to get 4,200 pounds. Put another way, you've lifted 105 pounds 40 times, for a total weight lifted of 4,200 pounds. Again, do not include weight lifted during your warm-up. The warm-up itself should not degenerate into a workout. Instead, utilize only the barest amount of energy and movement required to thoroughly warm up the joints, muscles, and connective tissues of the body parts you're going to be training, and perform only enough sets to obtain a *slight* pump and achieve viscosity in the joints.

For example, start out with just the empty bar you're about to utilize, and perform 1 to 2 sets of fairly high (20 to 30) repetitions with it. Then add what for you is some appreciable resistance, and perform two more sets of moderate reps (i.e., 10 to 20). Add weight again and, if needed, perform 1 to 2 more sets. You should be adequately warmed up by this point and ready to start your real sets. For the sake of consistency, try to always use the same warm-up routine.

5. The Total Weight per exercise is calculated by adding the Subtotal weights per set.

6. The Exercise Time is calculated from the time you start each individual exercise to the time you finish. It should always include the time you rest between sets. It should not include warm-up time. You will find a stopwatch very helpful for measuring this time.

7. The Power Factor is calculated by dividing the Total Weight by the time it took to lift it. So if you lift 16,730 pounds in 7½ minutes, your Power Factor is 2,231 pounds per minute ($16,730 \div 7½ = 2,231$). This is the power output of your muscles, on average, every minute you lifted 2,231 pounds. If you can increase that number on your next workout, you will know that you have increased the overload and gained strength.

8. The Power Index is calculated by multiplying the Total Weight by the Power Factor and dividing the product by 1,000,000. The significance of the Power Index will be discussed below.

9. The Total Weight in the Overall Workout Performance section is calculated by adding the Total Weight from each exercise (i.e., $16,730 + 13,040 + 8,940 + 72,785 + 72,680 = 184,175$ pounds). It represents the total amount of weight you lifted during your workout.

10. The Power Factor for Overall Workout Performance is calculated by dividing the Total Weight by the Total Time.

11. The Power Index for Overall Workout Performance is calculated by multiplying the Total Weight by the Power Factor and dividing the product by 1,000,000.

The Power Factor measures the amount of weight lifted (in pounds) in the amount of time (in minutes) that it takes to do the lifting. The Power Factor is expressed in pounds per minute (lbs/min). It is elegantly simple, yet profound in its result; it measures the muscular output of every exercise you perform! Once a means of quantifying muscular output is achieved, it gives the strength athlete the ability to clearly compare the effectiveness of altering factors such as number of reps per set, number of sets per exercise, slower or faster timing, lighter weights versus heavier weights, number of days off between workouts, steak and eggs versus oatmeal breakfasts.

THE POWER INDEX

The fact is, there are two ways you can get stronger. If you lift 2,000 pounds per minute today, and last workout you lifted only 1,700 pounds per minute, then you are stronger. However, if you lifted 1,700 pounds per minute for 5 minutes last workout, and this workout you lifted 1,700 pounds per minute for 7 minutes, you are also stronger, even though your Power Factor did not change. Why? Physics, again. If an engine (your muscles) can continue lifting at a certain rate, but for a longer period of time, it has to be stronger. You can't get something for nothing; more work done requires more strength.

As your Precision Training progresses you will become familiar with the two ways to achieve higher and higher Power Factors. Basically, you can either lift more total weight, or you can lift the same weight in a shorter period of time. While both achievements represent an increase in muscular output, the tactic of constantly trying to work out in less time has obvious limitations. For one thing, the quicker your workout pace, the greater the likelihood of injury. Also, constantly reducing the time of your workout will lead to the ridiculous: a 1-second workout per exercise. That won't tax your muscle's ability to generate its maximum power. Remember, being able to lift at the same rate but for a longer period of time is also an indication of increased strength.

It should be noted that you can achieve an extremely high Power Factor rating by performing certain exercises over a very short period of time. For example, suppose that you perform 6 calf raises with 500 pounds in 6 seconds. Your Power Factor, based on a pounds per minute average, would be a staggering 30,000 pounds per minute! Of course, you didn't really lift 30,000 pounds, nor did you work out for 1 minute, but your rate of lifting for one-tenth of a minute would be 30,000 pounds/minute! This is the limitation of looking at Power Factor numbers in isolation. Theoretically, you could increase your Power Factor every workout by using the above tactic, but you'd be cheating yourself. Enter the Power Index.

The Power Index is a mathematical function of the Total Weight lifted and the Power Factor. It is constructed to simultaneously reflect both the total weight you lift and the rate of your lifting. Since the Power Index is calculated by multiplying the Total Weight by the Power Factor, the weight component of your workout is actually squared. This produces a very large number which is then divided by 1,000,000 in order to make it more manageable.

Using the above example of six 500-pound calf raises in 6 seconds (30,000 Power Factor), the Power Index would be only 90 (3,000 lbs × 30,000 lbs/min ÷ 1,000,000). In contrast, during the development of this system, the authors were routinely achieving Power Indexes in calf raises of well over 4,500!

The Power Index is graphed on a logarithmic scale

because it involves squaring the total weight lifted. Consequently, the increases can be disproportionate both in raw numbers and in percentages; a modest increase in strength can yield a large increase in the Power Index. The only important element is that the trend be in an upward direction. That is an indication of improvement and enough to guide you in the direction of progress. You can't cheat the Power Index. The only way to make big gains in your Power Index is to work towards lifting at a high Power Factor and to keep it up for as long as you can. In short, you must maintain a high muscular output (i.e., pounds per minute ratio) for as long as possible.

The Power Index gives you a clear indication of whether or not your strength is increasing by measuring your capacity to continue lifting at the same rate but for a longer time. The Power Factor gives you a clear indication of whether or not your strength is increasing by measuring your capacity to lift at a higher rate. Those are the only two ways your muscles (or any engine) can get stronger. By monitoring these two numbers, you will have instant feedback as to which exercises and techniques yield results and which do not. You can also instantly spot overtraining or a plateau. The efficiency of this system is what makes it revolutionary. As you will see, the gains you stand to make from doing so are spectacular.

THE MILLION-POUND CLUB

In 1992, when we first began developing the Power Factor Training system, which uses the strongest range technique described in Section 2 of Precision Training, our performances were nothing spectacular, to be sure.

A typical workout of shoulders and arms, consisting of three different exercises, yielded an Overall Workout Performance of a 343 Power Factor and a 5.3 Power Index. Similarly, a chest, back, and legs workout, consisting of three different exercises, yielded an 848 Power Factor and a 36 Power Index.

It was at this point that the twofold benefit of strongest range of motion exercise com-

During the authors' Million-Pound Workout our Power Factor was equivalent to lifting two Lincoln Continentals every minute!

bined with the exact monitoring of muscular power output (to avoid both wasted effort and overtraining) led to an explosion of improvement. We were able to add more exercises to our workouts, and more weight to each exercise. After 52 days on the program (comprised of only 16 workouts), our shoulder and arm workouts yielded a 3,948 Power Factor and a 1,387 Power Index. Our chest, back, and leg workouts now yielded a 6,423 Power Factor and a 3,713 Power Index! Workouts that had begun with bench presses, shrugs, and leg presses of 175 pounds, 135 pounds, and 450 pounds, respectively, were up to an astounding 500 pounds, 540 pounds, and 1,325 pounds, respectively! And these were not single-repetition weights. These were sweet spot workout weights that we used to perform many sets of multiple repetitions.

On the 40th day of the program we arranged a special test of the system. We took a couple of extra days of rest, and were careful to carb up with the proper foods. We designed a special workout that combined upper and lower body parts and performed, in effect, a whole body workout. We used the bench press, deadlift, barbell shrug, leg press, and toe press and, in 131 minutes, we each lifted 1,000,375 pounds. This yielded a Power Factor of 7,636 pounds per minute, and a Power Index of 7,639! That Power Factor is equivalent to lifting two Lincoln Continentals every minute! Further, we kept that pace up for 2 hours and 11 minutes! This clearly and convincingly demonstrates the fantastic muscle- and strength-building capacity and efficiency of the system.

4

MONITORING YOUR RESULTS

The most significant ramification of the innovation of the Power Factor and Power Index is the ability, for the first time in the history of strength training, to provide a simple and mathematically precise indication of muscular output. Once this ability is established, it permits the most effective and efficient way to objectively measure your progress. Theories, myths, folklore, and science can all be put to the ultimate laboratory tests: How much overload does it deliver to the muscles? Does it develop greater strength? How much? How fast?

And this is just the tip of the proverbial iceberg. Henceforth, every factor that contributes to or detracts from your progress can now also be measured. You will be able to accurately measure the effect of increasing and decreasing reps, sets, weights, duration of workout, days off between workouts, using different dietary supplements, varying other aspects of your diet, and more. In the domain of bodybuilding, powerlifting, or any other form of strength training, such instant and precise assessment is nothing short of revolutionary! No longer is it necessary for the strength athletes to measure their progress by feel or instinct. And all you need to unleash this powerful new technology is a logbook and a stopwatch — common items in virtually every other sport, and yet so crucial to determining and plotting progress.

Could you imagine, for example, an Olympic miler trying to monitor his progress by feel or instinct while experimenting with different running techniques like wind sprints, intervals, running hills, etc. — and never measuring his progress with a stopwatch? Never having any tangible, objective measurement of the effects of his training techniques, nor of his improvement from one month to the next? Yet this is exactly the type of low-tech methodology that strength athletes have always used.

No longer is it necessary to measure progress by "feel" or "instinct." And all you need to unleash this powerful new technology is a logbook and a stopwatch.

WRITE IT DOWN

During your Precision Training workouts you will record the time, sets, reps, and weights that you lift on the Workout Record form. After you perform a workout you will record your results for each individual exercise on the Exercise Record form, and your overall workout performance on the Overall Performance Record form. The only calculation you need to carry out on the Exercise Record and Overall Performance Record forms is the percentage of change from workout to workout. This is accomplished in two simple steps:

1. New number – old number = difference
2. Difference ÷ old number × 100% = % change

For example, suppose your Power Factor goes from 1,675 to 1,890.

1. 1,890 – 1,675 = 215
2. 215 ÷ 1,675 = .128 × 100% = 12.8%

PLANNING AHEAD

One of the most powerful aspects of Precision Training is that it allows you to plan a workout ahead of time in order to achieve a target goal. The calculations necessary to do this are fairly simple; and we encourage you to familiarize yourself with the technique, since it is the key to guaranteeing that *every* workout is effective, efficient, and progressive. *Keep in mind that the two keys to maximum overload are total weight and time. These are the only factors you will adjust in your workouts.*

To illustrate, using the bench press numbers from the example entry on July 16 (shown on page 40), we see that the Total Weight lifted was 13,040 pounds and the Power Factor was 1,581 pounds/minute. Of course you would already know how long it took you to perform this exercise by looking at the Workout Record, but you could also get the time by dividing the Total Weight by the Power Factor (13,040 pounds divided by 1,581 pounds/minute = 8.25 minutes).

Now, suppose you set a goal of achieving a 20% increase in your Total Weight and a 10% increase in your Power Factor the next time you perform the bench press. Simply follow these steps:

1. Add 20% to 13,040 pounds (13,040 pounds × 1.20 = 15,650 pounds).

2. Add 10% to 1,581 pounds/minute (1,581 × 1.10 = 1,739 pounds/minute).

3. Divide the goal Total Weight by the goal Power Factor to determine the time allowed to perform the lifting (15,650 pounds ÷ 1,739 pounds/minute = 9.0 minutes).

	Total Weight	Power Factor	Time
	13,040 lbs	1,581 lbs/min	8.25 min
Goals:	15,650 lbs	1,739 lbs/min	9.0 min

By making these simple calculations, you now know exactly what you have to do in your next workout to ensure that your muscular output (i.e., overload) is higher: You have to lift 15,650 pounds in 9.0 minutes.

You can achieve your goal Total Weight simply by increasing your bench press pounds per minute output ratio (i.e., Power Factor) by adding an extra set or more reps to each set, or by using a heavier weight so that the total will be 15,650 pounds. As you work out, keep an eye on your stopwatch to ensure that you don't go over the 9.0 minutes you've set as your target time, and you will be certain that your Power Factor and Power Index have increased.

Here is one of the most important things to keep in mind: Ideally, no two workouts should ever be the same, because each time you return to the gym you have a new body. If your last workout was properly engineered, it stimulated muscle growth, and if you allowed yourself the required time for recovery and growth, you are a stronger person when you return to the gym. Therefore, performing the same workout as last time is useless. Since your muscles are now capable of more output, the old workout will not trigger any growth response. Get it? That's what "progressive overload" is all about. *Do the same workout every time and you get nowhere. Engineer an ever-increasing overload and you get steadily stronger.* The engineering is done with the Power Factor and Power Index numbers.

Goals can be set for one or all exercises you perform, and for your Total Workout as well. It is difficult to overstate the tremendous value of this ability of planning every workout to ensure that it is productive. This is the element of Precision Training that creates its unique efficiency, and it is the reason such a high percentage of trainees who use the system can work out once a week — or less — and still see consistent improvement, all the way to the optimum level of muscularity that they desire. *Every workout is a positive step toward the trainee's ultimate goal.*

Compare this to the old systems, where everyone follows a prescribed chart of exercises for six weeks, then switches to another chart for six more weeks, and so on — with every trainee using the same daily schedule and repetition schemes, regardless of the fact that there is a huge variation between individuals (remember the sweet spot?). Precision Training gives you the ability to engineer every workout that you perform to be maximally productive for *your* physiology.

GRAPH YOUR RESULTS

This technique of scientifically planning your goals ahead of time, and monitoring your results, permits the highest possible muscular overload each workout, and the greatest possible gains in size and strength. You will easily be able to see your progress by plotting your Power Factor and Power Index numbers on the graph paper located in your logbook. The trend that you should see on the graph is a consistent increase in your Power Factor and Power Index numbers, both on individual exercises and on your Overall Workout.

From time to time a workout may not yield an increase, and you may even see a decrease in your numbers. This, as you will discover, can be caused by a variety of circumstances. You may have worked out after not eating enough complex carbohydrates, or after not getting enough sleep, or when you were unable to concentrate due to stress. However, the #1 cause of a prolonged inability to improve is overtraining. Much more will be said about this crucial point later in this book, but for now it is critical to remember that muscular growth takes place only after you have recovered from your last workout, and the recovery and growth processes each require time to complete themselves. If you do not allow for this fact, your muscles cannot grow.

The following graph reflects one trainee's change in his Overall Workout Power Index during a period of 20 workouts over 60 days. As you can see, progress was steady on a Monday–Wednesday–Friday schedule, but by the 12th day a decline in the Power Index occurred. By switching to a two-day-per-week schedule, the trainee's metabolism was given the required time, not only to recover, but to increase its muscle mass. On a twice-a-week schedule, tremendous gains were made up to the 37th day. At this point, rather than just hitting a plateau, a sharp decrease occurred in his muscular output. Once again, this was corrected by adding more time off between workouts and, as expected, his Power Index again showed a tremendous improvement.

Note that the change in Power Index from Day 1 to Day 59 is enormous. This reflects a big increase in both the total amount of weight lifted and the rate of lifting (lbs/min). Such numerical gains can only be achieved through a big increase in muscular strength, and therefore create a corresponding increase in muscular size. Even subtle changes in the athlete's performance can be quickly and graphically identified and corrected through proper alterations in the workout and/or the training schedule. Precision Training identifies and prevents the chronic plateaus and overtraining that plague strength athletes who rely on the crude gauge of feel and instinct to measure their performance.

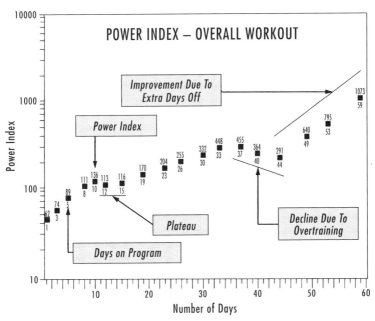

DEADLIFT   EXERCISE/OVERALL PERFORMANCE RECORD

Date	Total Weight	% Change	Power Factor	% Change	Power Index	+ OR − Change
7/16	16,730		2230		37.3	
7/23	18,070	+ 8 %	2310	+3.6 %	41.7	+ 4.4
7/30	19,010	+5.2 %	2430	+5.2 %	46.2	+ 4.5
8/6	21,960	+15.5 %	2718	+11.9 %	59.7	+13.5
8/11	19,480	−11.3 %	2460	−9.5 %	47.9	−11.8
8/21	22,640	+16.2 %	2814	+14.4 %	63.7	+15.8

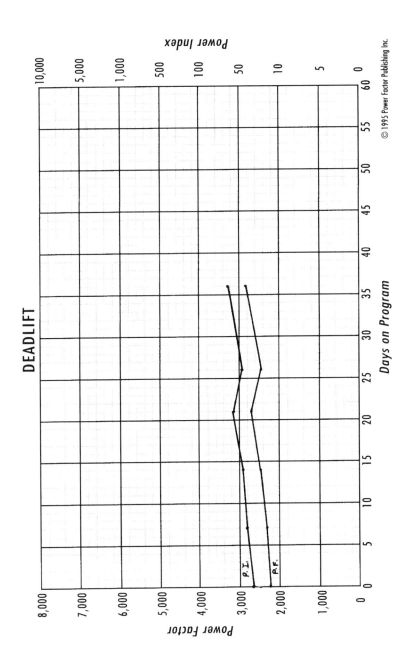

CHAPTER

5

THE TEN BEST EXERCISES FOR PRECISION TRAINING

WHAT IS FUNCTIONAL STRENGTH?

When most athletes go looking for a book on strength training, they usually find a book written for bodybuilders. The problem is that a bodybuilder has different training goals and motivations than any other athlete. For example, a guy who wants to paddle his kayak with more authority needs to increase his muscular strength, but he doesn't want to train four days a week with routines that involve four exercises per body part and take two hours to complete. In short, he does not want to become a bodybuilder just to become a better kayaker.

Further, all the kayaker needs is functional strength; that is, strength in his normal range of motion for his sport. Functional strength is what you use naturally. For example, when you push a car, your arms are extended most of the way out in front of you because that is your strongest range. If you held your hands against your chest while pushing you could not use nearly as much power. Bodybuilders care about the actual shape of their muscles, and spend a tremendous amount of time and effort doing exercises they believe (often incorrectly) will create their desired shaping effect. Frankly, many of these exercises are a waste of time for people who want better muscle tone and increased strength for the purpose of everyday activities or for a specific sport that uses strength within normal functional ranges. If you want better flexibility, do stretching and yoga exercises. If you want more strength, lift weights. Doing both at the same time will only minimize your results in both areas.

COMPOUND MOVEMENTS

Precision Training avoids the unproductive exercises by utilizing the best "compound movements" that generate the highest Power Factor and Power Index numbers of which you are capable. Compound movements involve two or more groups of muscles working in concert to perform a task. It is the way your body naturally creates movement. For example, the leg press exercise involves the quadriceps, the hamstrings, and the gluteus muscles.

Devising ways of training each of these muscles separately is a waste of time, and the Power Factor and Power Index numbers of these isolation exercises prove it. Be glad there are exercises that hit several muscles at once; these deliver the highest Power Factors and Power Indexes and trigger your central nervous system to initiate the growth process.

After experimenting with many different exercises and crunching the numbers through the Power Factor and Power Index computation formulas, we found that the following 10 exercises yield the biggest gains in functional strength *and* highest pounds per minute of overload.

1. DEADLIFT

This is the best exercise you can perform for increasing the size and strength of your lower back, buttocks, and hamstrings. These are the muscles that will serve you well if you happen to be an athlete looking to sharpen your tennis, skiing, golf, basketball, football, hockey, wrestling, or baseball skills. Always keep a slight bend in your knees when performing this exercise to ensure that your lumbar muscles, rather than your vertebrae, bear the brunt of the exercise stress.

Starting position: Place a barbell on the floor in front of you, and grasp the barbell with a grip of approximately shoulder width. Your feet should be under the bar. Slowly pull upward, making sure to keep your arms straight, until you are fully erect and the barbell is resting on your upper thighs.

Deadlift – Starting Position

Movement: Lower the barbell smoothly, bending at the waist while keeping a slight bend in your knees, until the weight has been returned to the floor. Then raise the weight back up to the starting position using only the power of your hamstrings, glutes, and lower back muscles.

Deadlift – Finish Position

2. BENCH PRESS

The bench press is a fundamental compound movement for the upper body that will build power, size, and strength into the pectorals, anterior deltoids, and tricep muscles. Once again, it's almost the perfect all-round sports exercise, since almost every sport requires functional strength development in its execution.

Bench Press – Starting Position

Starting position: Lie back on a flat bench, with a barbell resting on the supports attached to the bench. Place your feet flat on the floor for balance. Your grip should be medium width, so that as you lower the bar, your forearms are straight up and down (vertical). Raise the barbell from the supports and lock it out directly above your chest.

Movement: With the bar directly above your chest, lower the resistance until it

Bench Press – Finish Position

touches your mid-chest. Then press the barbell upward until your arms are fully locked out again.

3. LAT PULLDOWNS

This exercise will widen your upper lats and put you well on your way to developing an incredible V-shape! When your strength increases, it also allows you to utilize more weight than your body weight, which, for overload purposes, is ideal!

Starting position: Taking a close, underhand grip on the bar, sit on the seat with your knees hooked under the support. Your arms should be stretched fully above your head, and the pull should be felt in both your lats and shoulder blades.

Movement: Pull the bar down until it touches your upper chest. Concentrate on making the upper back do the work, and don't lean back to involve the lower back muscles. Then release the contraction, and make a point of feeling the lats return to the fully stretched position.

Lat Pulldown – Start Position

Lat Pulldown – Finish Position

4. SQUATS

Without question, squats are one of the most results-producing exercises in existence. Whether you need to firm up your thighs, hamstrings, and glutes, or want to really pack on the muscle, squats will do it for you. This is the most effective leg-building exercise you can perform with barbells.

Starting position: To perform the squat properly, stand erect with a barbell across your shoulders. If you're lifting the barbell off squat stands or the pins in a power rack, step back until you clear the supports, and then steady your stance.

Squat
— Starting Position

Movement: Taking a deep breath, bend your knees and lower your body until your thighs are slightly below 90 degrees. As soon as you reach the bottom position, rise immediately, under full control, while exhaling. Keep your head up and your eyes looking straight ahead at all times. Inhale when you reach the top, and repeat the movement.

Squat
— Finish Position

5. STANDING BARBELL PRESSES

The standing barbell press is a movement that will build extremely powerful ligaments and tendons, and increase the size of the muscles in your deltoids, traps, and upper back.

Starting position: Lift a barbell to shoulder level and, in a standing position, with your hands approximately three inches wider on each side than your shoulders, press the barbell upward until your elbows are locked.

Movement: Lower the bar back down until it is touching your upper chest. Dip your legs in a simulated split position (i.e., one knee just slightly forward and unlocked, while the back leg remains slightly bent). From this lowered position, push/press the weight to the fully extended position, using slight assistance from your calves and quads. This is really just a slight dipping movement, designed to assist you in pressing that heavy weight upwards.

Standing Barbell Press – Starting Position

Standing Barbell Press – Finish Position

6. CLOSE-GRIP BENCH PRESSES

This exercise will place a tremendous overload on the triceps and will also involve the pectorals and anterior deltoids.

Starting position: Take a narrow grip in the middle of a barbell (the outside of your palms should be just touching the inside of the knurling). Then, lying on your back on an exercise bench, raise the barbell off the supports and extend your arms upward until they are completely locked out.

Movement: Lower the barbell until it nearly touches your chest, then push it back up to the starting position. Try to get a good cadence ("rep speed") going with this exercise.

Close-Grip Bench Presses
– Starting Position

Close-Grip Bench Presses
– Finish Position

7. BARBELL SHRUGS

This exercise directly involves the trapezius muscles of your upper back, as well as your entire shoulder structure. The combined muscular effect will enable you to move some tremendous poundages.

Starting position: Take an overhand grip on a barbell and stand erect. Your hands should be slightly wider apart than your shoulders. It is strongly recommended that you get yourself a pair of heavy-duty lifting hooks, as the weight you'll be hoisting in this movement will mount up very quickly.

Barbell Shrugs – Starting Position

Barbell Shrugs – Finish Position

Movement: Shrug your shoulders upward as quickly as possible, with no pause at either the top or the bottom of the movement. Make sure to keep your elbows straight at all times so that your traps alone, and not your biceps, are doing the work. Do not move so fast that inertia or gravity does the work. Keep the weight under your full control at all times.

8. STANDING BARBELL CURLS

Standing barbell curls provide tremendous overload to the bicep muscles of your upper arms primarily, and to your brachialis and forearm muscles secondarily.

Starting position: Take a shoulder-width underhanded grip on either a cambered or regular barbell. Anchor your elbows firmly into your sides, and keep them there throughout the exercise.

Movement: Slowly raise the barbell upward until you reach a position of full contraction. Then immediately reverse the procedure, lowering the barbell slowly and under full control back to the starting position.

Standing Barbell Curls – Starting Position

Standing Barbell Curls – Finish Position

9. STANDING CALF RAISES WITH A BARBELL

This is a wonderful exercise for the gastrocnemius (calf) and associated muscles of the lower leg, making it excellent training for any sport involving running.

Starting position: Take an overhand grip on the barbell and stand erect. Rest the bar against your thighs and steady your stance.

Movement: Keeping your legs straight, rise up on the balls of your feet until your calves are maximally contracted. Hold this fully contracted position and then lower your heels back to the starting position.

Standing Calf Raises –
Starting Position

Standing Calf Raises –
Finish Position

10. CRUNCHES

A strong abdomen is absolutely crucial to the successful performance of any sport. While several of the exercises just described will involve the abdominal muscles, crunches are ideal to target these muscles specifically. Since this exercise uses no additional weight (except as described in Section 2), use 25% of your body weight as the weight in the Power Factor and Power Index calculations.

Starting position: Lie on your back on the floor, and place your feet on top of a bench; or lie on a bench with your knees bent. Place your hands behind your head.

Crunches – Starting Position

Movement: Try to keep your chin on your chest, and slowly curl your trunk upward towards a sitting position. You'll find that you can only curl up a third of the range you would be able to achieve if you were performing a normal sit-up. This is fine, because that is all the range of motion your abdominals require to be stimulated into growth. Once you've ascended to a fully contracted position, hold the position for a two-count, then slowly lower yourself back to the starting position. Repeat for the required number of repetitions.

Crunches – Finish Position

THE ROUTINE

If you train properly you'll be amazed at the transformation that will take place in your physique in just a few weeks. The reason is that weight training is an extremely powerful catalyst that forces your body into virtually instant response. The harder you train, the faster your body overcompensates in the form of additional muscle mass, but the harder you train, the more rest and recuperation your body requires in order to bring about the physiological renovations in your physique.

The good news is that, as you get bigger and stronger, your workouts will, of necessity, have to be spaced further and further apart. Don't be surprised if, in the near future, you find yourself working out a mere four times a month. In fact, once you reach what you consider to be your optimum level of muscularity, and this is purely subjective (as a golfer's optimum level of muscularity would be far below what would be acceptable to a professional bodybuilder), you simply have to switch to a "maintenance" mode in which you may work out a mere two days per month. This may sound incredible but, as you'll read elsewhere in this manual, the verdict is in; people need a lot less strength training than was originally believed to be the case.

This routine is to be initially performed on alternate days. For example, Mondays, Wednesdays and Fridays. Under no circumstances should you attempt to train more than three days a week and never should you attempt to get all three workouts in by training three days in a row! The alternate day schedule is set up this way for a reason: Physiologists have determined that, at the beginning of a training program, most people's bodies will require a minimum of 48 hours of rest in between workouts to recover from both the training session and for the muscular subsystems to overcompensate from the stressor by creating increased muscle mass. As you become stronger, you'll find that the amount of time you require between workouts will increase dramatically, particularly if you begin incorporating the advanced Precision Training technique of strongest-range repetitions in Section Two of this manual. The whole key to success is to train by the numbers. If your Power Factor and Power Index numbers are constantly climbing, then you're on the right track. The moment they plateau, it's time to back off on the frequency of your workouts. Your success depends almost exclusively upon the proper execution of the exercises in this routine, and the proper calculation of each exercise's Power Factor and Power Index.

Make the effort to insure that correct form is always employed during the performance of the exercises. Since the beginner's workout consists of full-range movements, the danger of injury exists in the weakest range of motion, so control over the movement is absolutely crucial. Never complete a movement too rapidly. It should be a muscular effort without the aid of momentum or gravity. Also, remember to start the stop watch as soon as you begin your first set. We've geared this routine around barbells because we want you to be able to perform this workout in the privacy of your own home if you so choose. Obviously, joining a health club offers a great deal more variety but, in all candor, you don't need any more equipment than is indicated in this routine to make dramatic gains in muscularity.

The number of sets and repetitions that we recommend below are for the purpose of getting started only. The most important element to remember is a steady increase in your Power Factor and Power Index numbers.

This will come about by experimenting with the combinations of weight on the bar, number of repetitions, and number of sets. Using a broad rule, most people quickly advance in strength to a point where their highest muscular output occurs in the range of four to seven sets of 20 to 35 repetitions. Also, most people achieve their highest overload by starting an exercise with a weight that is 50% to 60% of the heaviest they can handle (their one rep maximum weight), performing one or two sets, then increasing the weight on the bar, and performing another one or two sets, and so on until the last set when they go to "failure" with a weight that is 80% to 95% of their maximum. "Failure" refers to performing repetitions until you simply cannot perform another rep. Remember though, these are guidelines that refer to a majority of people but, by no means, to all people. Be sure to experiment to see where your personal "sweet spot" exists.

The great majority of questions we receive from trainees can be answered by asking one question: "will this technique increase my Power Factor and/or Power Index?" For example, common questions are: "Can I perform dips instead of close grip bench presses?" "Can I train my legs on a completely separate day by creating a Workout C?" "Can I train every 5 days?" or "Can I perform every set at the same weight?" To all of these questions the answer is: Will it cause your Power Factor and/or Power Index numbers to increase or decrease? An increase is good, a decrease is bad; nothing else matters! Remember that.

WORKOUT A

When starting out perform three sets of 15 repetitions for each of the following exercises:

- Shoulder Press
- Barbell Shrugs
- Close Grip Bench Press
- Barbell Curls
- Crunches

WORKOUT B

When starting out perform three sets of 15 repetitions for each of the following exercises:
- Deadlifts
- Bench Press
- Lat Pulldowns
- Squats
- Toe Raises

TIME KEEPING

There are two general rules for keeping track of your workouts:

1. Don't time your warm-up routine.
2. Time everything else.

Since time is half of the muscular overload equation it is critical to measure it properly. To measure your entire workout keep track of what time you start and what time you finish. Typically, this will be 30 to 60 minutes. Also measure the time it takes to perform each of the five exercises that you will do in your workout. For example 8½ minutes for bench presses and 7¼ minutes for deadlifts. Start your stopwatch when you begin your first set and don't stop it until the end of your last set even if you go get a drink of water or answer the phone. Your Power Factor and Power Index are zero when you are resting and that fact has to be averaged into your calculations. Remember, if you lift the same total weight but do it one minute faster than last time, you are stronger. However, you will only recognize the improvement if you have kept proper track of time. The time taken in between exercises does not have to be measured separately because it will appear in the start and finish times of your entire workout — the Overall Workout.

Perform your warm-up exercises as a completely separate endeavor. Do not include the time and do not include the weight. The warm-up is a safety precaution to help prevent injuries. The warm-up is low intensity, performed with light weights, and is not intended to stimulate muscle growth so please don't try to turn it into something it is not meant to be. Whether you warm up all muscles before your workout or each muscle group just before a particular exercise is a matter of personal preference. As long as you are consistent from workout to workout your Power Factor and Power Index numbers will still reflect your progress, or lack thereof, since the identical warm-up will automatically factor out of each workout.

6

PRECISION TRAINING FOR WOMEN

TARGETING THOSE "PROBLEM" AREAS

Many women still believe that if they engage in any kind of strength training they're going to end up with large, unfeminine muscles. Let us explode that myth right now. It all harkens back to Chapter 2 where we touched on the significance of genetics in determining the ultimate mass potential of an individual's physique. It should be pointed out that less than 1% of the male population has the capacity to develop a massive musculature like that of a professional bodybuilder and, likewise, 99% of women lack the requisite genetics to develop a body like the current Ms. Olympia — even if they wanted to.

The reason men are bigger and stronger than women is also genetically based — because of the male hormone testosterone, which operates on the growth mechanism of the male body. The small percentage of women who have large muscles have either inherited a genetic predisposition toward muscle mass or have an unusually high quantity of testosterone in their system. While the adrenal and sex glands of women do secrete a small amount of testosterone, it isn't enough to provide for much in the way of muscular development. The truth is, even though the majority of women couldn't develop really large muscles if their lives depended on it, every woman can benefit from vigorous, intense weight training.

While the body weight of the typical male is approximately 15% fat, the typical female body weight is comprised of 25% fat. This difference in body fat levels is due, in part, to the fact

The best procedure for promoting weight loss and altering body composition for improved appearance is a combination of diet and increased muscular output.

that female hormones, particularly estrogen, promote fat storage. It's also true, however, that women traditionally have been discouraged from participating in athletics and overloading their muscles vigorously. As a result, most women never develop much in the way of strength or muscle tone. This is unfortunate because bodies of sedentary people, male or female, continue to change composition as they grow older, primarily with the addition of fat. This means that more of the total body weight will be fatty tissue and less will be lean body mass or muscle tissue, and it is this progressive loss of muscle tissue that makes it more and more difficult to lose fat. This results in a cycle that's hard to change — particularly for women.

Men naturally have more lean body mass and less fat to start with because of a higher basal metabolic rate or BMR (anywhere from 5% to 20% higher than women). Although some of the male's leanness may be a sexual characteristic, it is the leaner people of either sex who have a higher BMR. This greater leanness means an ability to accommodate greater caloric intake without adding fat tissue to the body, and it also serves to facilitate the burning of fat. Muscle tissue is much more active than fat tissue, burning more calories even at rest. So while lowcalorie diets may result in weight loss, they are more effective when combined with exercise that strengthens and tones muscle.

Studies have revealed that 25% to 90% of the weight loss resulting from dietary restriction alone comes from muscle tissues, organs, and fluid but not from fat. This loss of protein from muscles and organs is difficult to prevent even with a small caloric restriction in an inactive person and explains the wrinkling and sagging tissues that so often accompany weight loss by diet. For some, increased activity alone will turn the tide. One study found that overweight college women lost an average of 5.3 pounds in a two-month period during which they participated in a four-day-a-week, one-hour-per-session exercise program without any dietary restrictions. Skin-fold measurements revealed that the weight loss was due to a much larger loss of fatty tissue and a simultaneous gain in muscle or lean body mass. Obviously then, the best procedure for promoting weight loss and altering body composition for improved appearance is a combination of diet and increased muscular output.

SELF ASSESSMENT

Of all the reasons women list for taking up an exercise and diet program, increasing sex appeal is still uppermost in the minds of a great majority. After all, vanity is a strong motive for most of us. In a world where you present yourself to others daily, looking good seems to be of paramount importance.

The woman who has been sedentary for any length of time doesn't need reminders that she is losing her shape. There are certain areas that sag, dimple, and expand, serving as stark visible reminders of physical deterioration and potentially declining sex appeal. More often than not, the encroachment of the cellulite look and sagging tissues is due to poor muscle tone that results from inadequate training. Proper training, such as that found within the pages of this manual, is part of the answer to regaining youthful form. Here are three trouble spots women need to watch, and some supplementary exercises that will help firm them:

Proper exercise will enhance your muscle tone and tighten your midsection.

THE WAISTLINE

Nothing seems to make a woman more painfully aware of her physical appearance than a bulging waistline. The first requisite in waist reduction is the elimination of excess fat. Reducing the fatty tissue circling the waist will come only from a reduction in the percentage of fat stored by the body and this is best accomplished, most safely, by reducing daily calorie intake while at the same time eating a well-balanced diet.

Reducing calories below maintenance levels will result in fat loss over the entire body and, if you're persistent with your diet, you'll ultimately see a dramatic reduction in the fat that is presently deposited around your waist. But keep in mind that fat used for energy while on a diet comes fairly uniformly from the body's multiple fat stores, never from any one isolated area like the waistline. And since fat loss is a relatively slow process at the best of times, it will take a while before significant results are seen.

The degree to which you reduce daily caloric intake can be varied according to individual needs, but a minimum reduction of five hundred calories per day is necessary to stimulate any meaningful fat loss. On the other hand, it's considered unwise for nutritional reasons to reduce one's daily intake to less than 1200 calories.

THE ROLE OF EXERCISE

While your diet is cutting into that unsightly flab, you'll have to turn to exercise in order to enhance your muscle tone and tighten your midsection. Don't think that you only have to target a problem area with one or two exercises to solve your problem. It's almost a natural tendency to think that spot reduction is possible. It isn't. Fat is general, and spot reduction just doesn't occur. Exercise, of course, raises your activity quotient and metabolic rate so that some body fat is used for energy.

Intensive physical conditioning exercises can cause a depletion in fat deposits and an increase in lean body weight. In fact, it's possible to maintain the same weight but change your body's composition with a decrease in body fat and a balancing increase in muscular tissue. For example, a woman who weighs 140 pounds at 40% body fat will look much leaner and fit at 140 pounds and 20% body fat. Regardless of what changes in body composition and fat reduction result from your increased energy expenditure, your waist — or any body part for that matter — will trim down only in direct proportion to the loss of overall body fat.

TARGETING THE WAIST

A tight midsection, with firm, defined muscles, is a readily attainable goal for the average woman. Whatever your present condition, once you get started, don't be discouraged. The combination of diet and exercise, if you are faithful to them, will soon create a healthier and more shapely appearance.

Crunches: Since we've described this exercise in the previous chapter, we won't go over its performance again here. Crunches will target your abdominal muscles directly, while overhead presses and standing barbell curls (also found in the previous chapter) will further involve the abdominals in an indirect way because they are required to contract statically for the purpose of stabilizing your torso during these lifts. If you want to strengthen the oblique muscles at the sides of your waist, feel free to add the next exercise to your routine.

Side Bends: To perform this movement correctly stand with your feet about shoulder width apart and clasp your hands behind your head. Keeping your legs straight, bend slowly to the left as far as possible, without leaning forward or backward, then return to the starting position and bend to the right. This exercise will tighten the sides of the waist by alternately stretching and contracting the oblique muscles. Repeat for 12 repetitions to each side and add four repetitions a day until you've reached 50. When you reach the point where you can knock off 50 reps per set, you're ready to add two components to your exercise: Resistance (in the form of a barbell plate) and a stop watch (in order to determine your Power Factor for this movement). Hold the barbell plate behind your head and repeat the exercise in the fashion described above.

THE GLUTES

Most women rarely get a good view of their gluteus muscles so it's easy for them to be unaware of their appearance. Because of the woman's naturally larger and

It is properly toned muscle tissue that gives your body shape and form.

broader pelvic girdle, in addition to her hormonal predisposition to fat buildup in the hips and buttocks, this area can quickly become out of condition. And the problem with the buttocks is that you can diet severely with little visible improvement.

The reason that diet alone can't turn the trick is that a sagging and deteriorating derriere is the result of diminished muscle tone in the gluteus muscles of the buttocks. While little can be done to change the shape of the bosom, there is always hope for the "glutes" (the name bodybuilders use in referring to the buttocks). It's possible to train away that so-called cellulite, and get rid of the dimples, pockmarks, and ripples that plague many women. A program of persistent, progressive muscular output exercise will do the job. Combined with a sensible diet, exercise can greatly tone and reshape the buttocks.

It is properly toned muscle tissue that gives your body shape and form. Fat has no tone or firmness at all. Since the buttocks problem is due to loss of muscle tissue itself, the only solution is to strengthen the entire area, including the gluteus muscles, rear thighs, and lower back. High-repetition flexibility exercises, like those seen in so many women's magazines, will do little to help because the intensity of muscular output is simply too low.

Progressive resistance exercises provided by barbells or exercise machines are necessary to develop and tighten the glutes. You don't need to perform a lot of sets of these movements when starting out. As a rule of thumb, stick with the two or three sets of 8 to 15 reps outlined in the previous chapters, but once you start to progress, you'll find that you may need to increase either your number of sets or repetitions, and most definitely the weights you use, in order to continue generating higher Power Factor and Power Index numbers (the only sure signal of progress taking place). No, it's not the easiest form of exercise but it is the only type that efficiently produces substantial results.

GLUTE AND THIGH EXERCISES

1. *Stiff-legged Deadlifts:* This version of deadlifts is more effective in targeting the glutes. With your ankles against the bar, knees locked straight and head looking up, grasp the bar with an overhand grip and stand erect with the bar straight down at arm's length. Pause momentarily, then lower the bar slowly back to the floor. This exercise works the entire back side of the body from head to toe and will do wonders for tightening this problem area.

Stiff-legged deadlifts, start position.

Stiff-legged deadlifts, finish position.

2. *Barbell Lunges:* These can actually be done with either dumbbells or barbells but this exercise is on par with squats for targeting the glutes, hips, thighs and hamstrings. Holding a barbell across your shoulders, stride forward with your left foot, then push yourself all the way back to the starting position in one step. Repeat with the right leg. If using dumbbells, hold them at arm's length at your side and do the same thing.

Barbell lunges, start position.

Barbell lunges, finish position.

3. *Leg Curls:* You will need a special machine for this one, but it is well worth it because leg curls are the

Leg curls, start position.

Leg curls, finish position.

most direct hamstring movement in existence — which is important if your desire is to firm up the rear portion of your legs. Lying on your stomach, position yourself so your Achilles tendons make contact with the padded movement arm. Under control, bend your knees and curl the lower legs until the pad hits your buttocks. Pause and lower slowly.

4. *Leg Extensions:* Again, you'll need a special machine for this movement (and you will for the next two as well), but this movement thrusts the resistance directly onto the quadricep muscles of the frontal thighs. Sit on the padded surface of the machine with your legs toward the movement arm of the apparatus. Slide forward until the backs of your knees are at the edge of the machine's padded surface. Hook your insteps under the lower set of roller pads. Sit erect and grasp the edges of the seat pad to steady your body in position during the movement. Slowly extend your legs until they are locked in a straight position and hold this position for a distinct pause before lowering the weight back to the starting position.

Leg extensions, start position.   Leg extensions, finish position.

5. *Hip Adduction/Abduction Machine:* When you force your thighs together using this machine, you are strongly stressing the adductor muscles of your inner thighs. When pushing your legs away from each other, under resistance using this machine, you stress the

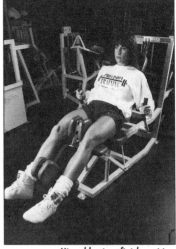

Hip adduction, start position.   *Hip adduction, finish position.*

muscles at the sides of your hips as well as the upper and outer thighs. Sit in the machine and recline against the backrest. Fasten the lap belt around your hips, and place your legs between the pads of the movement arms. A rotating level at the side of the machine will allow you to select the direction from which you apply resistance. This should be set to the correct selection before entering the machine. From this position, with your legs completely spread apart, slowly force them closed against the resistance provided by the machine. Or, with the lever set to the opposite selection, you can force your legs apart from a together position at the start of the movement.

THE BUST

Testimony to women's preoccupation with the appearance of their bust line are the lucrative businesses that purport to be responding to their "needs." Gimmicks of all sorts can be found at the back of most women's magazine. There are exercises that promise added inches, and creams and massage treatments that are said to stimulate growth.

Our advice is to forget about these gimmicks and be realistic. Be prepared to spend a little time on yourself. First, you'll have to accept the fact that the size and shape of your bust are inherited features and, therefore, not subject to dramatic alteration. Very little can be done to change the size and shape of the bust outside

The size and shape of your bust are inherited features and, therefore, not subject to dramatic alteration.

of drug treatments, surgery, implants or large increases or decreases in body fat. However, having said that, you can decide to bring your bust up to its potential which, of course, involves exercise. The bench press exercise outlined in Chapter 5 is the best exercise for improving the size of your chest because it allows you to generate your highest Power Factor and Power Index numbers. However, should you wish to utilize a different exercise to target the same area, feel free to substitute one of the following:

Dumbbell Flyes: Compared to bench presses, dumbbell flyes performed on a flat bench are an isolation movement. Flyes will isolate the exercise stress primarily on the pectoral muscles and anterior deltoids, with minimum stress on the remainder of the deltoid muscle complex and the triceps. Grasp two moderately weighted dumbbells and sit at the end of a flat exercise bench. Place your feet solidly on the floor on either side

Dumbbell Flyes, start position.

Dumbbell Flyes, finish position.

of the bench, then lie back on the flat surface of the bench, extending your arms straight upward from your shoulders. Rotate your wrists so your palms are facing each other and press the dumbbells together directly above your chest. Bend your elbows at approximately 15 degree angles and maintain them in this rounded posture throughout your set. Keeping your arms rounded, slowly lower the dumbbells directly out to the sides and downward in semicircular arcs until they are below the level of your chest and your pectoral muscles are mildly stretched. At this point, reverse the movement of the dumbbells, using only the strength of your chest muscles to pull them back along the same arc to the starting position.

The Pec Dec Machine: This exercise hits not only your chest but also your anterior deltoids and serratus muscles. Adjust the height of the machine's seat so your upper arms are perpendicular to your torso when you place your forearms against the resistance lever pads in front of you. Your feet should be set comfortably on the floor (don't press up with your toes or have the seat set too high). Starting from a position where your arms are comfortably stretched back, slowly draw your elbows forward until they meet directly in front of your torso. Hold this fully contracted position for a two-count then lower the resistance slowly back to the starting position. It's important to remember that most women simply will not develop muscular mass no matter what they do, but that lack of bulk doesn't mean that strength and tone are not improving. And don't forget the other advantages of proper strength training reduced chances of developing osteoporosis in later years, reduced body fat levels, improved endurance, increased metabolic rate and an enhanced self-image.

Pec Dec, start position.   *Pec Dec, finish position.*

7

RECOVERY ABILITY – THE FORGOTTEN FACTOR

THE GROWTH PROCESS

Exercise physiologists have found that strength increases occur only when the athlete's amount of training and recovery ability are in balance. Because this balance is both delicate and elusive, it can be established and sustained only if you understand the intricacies involved in the tri-phasic process of recuperation.

Phase One of systemic recovery takes place in the minutes and hours immediately after an intense workout. Some exercise physiologists have theorized that within as little as three seconds after a muscle has been worked to a point of momentary muscular failure, it can recover a substantial portion of the strength it had lost as a result of the exercise. It is during this immediate phase, that most of the local energy reserves utilized in the actual training effort are replenished. This does not mean, however, that the muscle will recover its full capacity, nor the deeper reserves of general adaptation energy, in six seconds or even in as many minutes.

When, and only when, this initial phase has been completed can the regeneration process begin the additional repair, growth and strengthening of the muscles themselves. The second phase is chemical in nature and it is rather time-consuming. Current research makes it clear that what had previously been considered a mandatory recovery period between workouts of 42-60 hours, may have missed the side of the barn by at least seven days. In some cases, up to six weeks may be required for Phase Two to run its course successfully depending, of course, on the type and amount of overload imposed on the system and individual recovery ability.

Phase Three, that of overcompensation or muscle growth, will only take place once the previous two phases have elapsed. What this means is that any additional training undertaken before Phases One and Two are complete will be with a muscular system that has been denied full recuperation and growth. If this approach is repeated regularly, strength will decrease. This is why allowing for adequate recovery and growth to occur is absolutely crucial to your continued progress.

THE TWO SIDES OF RECOVERY

Like all other physical characteristics of humans, recovery ability after exercise varies widely between individuals. After identical workouts, one person may be able to return to the gym in 48 hours and see an increase in his Power Factor and Power Index while another person may need a full week in order to recover sufficiently and show improvement.

When you use Precision Training you will have the ability to see the extent to which you have recovered

Strength increases occur only when the athlete's amount of training and recovery ability are in balance.

from your Power Factor and Power Index numbers. If you return to the gym too soon after a workout you will not perform as well and your numbers will reflect this. When this happens, just add a day or two of recovery until your numbers show some improvement. As alluded to earlier, this new found ability led us to an entirely different perspective on recovery ability. During the development of Precision Training it became necessary, for a variety of reasons, for both of us to take six weeks off from working out. When we finally returned to the gym we were mentally prepared for a light workout. To our surprise we discovered that as the workout progressed, we not only had no sign of atrophy but our strength had taken a quantum leap upwards. We both set new personal records in every lift we performed.

It is clear that recovery can be measured along a range of time that begins with the first day you can return to the gym expecting an improvement and ends with the last day you can return to the gym expecting an improvement. Precision Training will allow you to precisely determine your personal range of recovery. Depending on a variety of personal factors your own range may be anywhere from two or three days to many weeks.

Consequently, if you are the sort of person who loves to train; that is, a person who wants to be in the gym as frequently as possible, you can work at the close end of your range of recovery scale by returning to the gym as soon as you are able. If, on the other hand, you have family or business commitments or an otherwise busy schedule, you can schedule your workouts further apart by working at the far end of your recovery range and working out as little as possible without losing ground by way of your Power a Factor and Power Index numbers. In either case, you'll make dramatic and consistent progress.

PROTRACTED RECOVERY PERIODS

The value of knowing your personal range of recovery ability is that you'll know, with mathematical precision, exactly when you honestly do have to train and when you don't. Just because somebody else can train three days a week and make progress is irrelevant in your personal training considerations; he may have stumbled on to a margin of training that falls within his range of personal recovery ability and is (for the moment at least) making progress. The problem will arise, however, when he eventually ceases to make progress. He won't know if his lack of progress is due to having reached the upper limits of his genetic potential, having become "stale," or training with insufficient intensity to continue the growth process.

On the other hand, when you know how many days it takes you to recover from having lifted "X" number of pounds in a given workout, then it stands to reason that it will take even more days to recover once you've increased your Power Factor. No longer do you need to entertain guilty thoughts because you didn't train one day last week. You would have been doing more harm than good to your strength and physique aspirations if you worked out even one day sooner than the first day your recovery ability had replenished itself.

What we've learned about recovery ability is that there exists a general and very limited supply, almost like a small reservoir, and every time you lift a weight, you dip a certain percentage into this reservoir. A percentage that must ultimately be replaced before the growth process can occur. Some exercise physiologists have theorized that while the average trainee has the potential to increase his starting level of strength some 300% within the first year of training, his ability to recover from such workouts increases by only 50%. This creates a fundamental challenge to the trainee as his rate of overloading his system increases at a different rate than his ability to recover from the overload. Think of it this way: Say that your body has the ability to recover from 100 "units" of exercise per day. When you start your training your strength is minimal and you may only be capable of generating 70 or 80 "units" of overload. No problem; your metabolic system can recover from that in one day. But as you grow stronger, your muscles have the ability to generate 150 "units" of overload which will take two days from which to recover. By the time your recovery ability begins to improve, your muscular output might be up to 300 to 350 "units" of overload and you must take multiple days off between workouts. This is a critical balance. The trainee who returns to the gym too soon will have a recovery deficit which has not been paid off in sufficient recovery "units" and will just dig himself a bigger hole from which to recuperate.

When you use Precision Training you will have the ability to see the extent to which you have recovered by noting your Power Factor and Power Index numbers. If you return to the gym too soon after a workout you will not perform as well and your numbers will reflect this. If this happens, just add a day or two of recovery until your numbers show some improvement.

MENTZER'S RESEARCH

At about the time we authors encountered our first plateau on the Precision Training system, former Mr. Universe, Mike Mentzer, called to inform us of the results of some recent research he had conducted over a two year period involving some 200 clients that had been training under his direct supervision. According to Mentzer: "I've noted with many of my clients that they're stronger after a two to three week layoff. I've noted this with all of my clients, some whom were either forced to take a lay off or had to for a variety of other reasons. Almost all of them expressed an anxiety of 'Geez, I'm afraid I'm going to lose my size and strength if I take time off from training,' but I've had these people take up to three weeks off and, with almost every single case, they've come back stronger. I even asked [Mr. Olympia] Dorian Yates whether or not he'd noted a similar phenomenon with regards to his own training experience and he said 'You know, Mike, it's true.' This is not just a minor point to be glossed over. I'm beginning to suspect this thing with frequency of training has a hell of a lot to do with a trainee's ulti-mate success. Maybe the solution would be to train each bodypart once very two weeks. Why not?" [7]

Why not indeed? As Mentzer has correctly pointed out in his articles in the Weider magazines (also in his revised Heavy Duty book), training progress should not be an unpredictable, hap hazard, irregular phenomenon. If you're training with sufficient overload to stimulate growth and if you're allowing what for you is adequate recovery time to take place, then you should be witnessing consistent improvement on a regular basis. Conversely, if you're training with inadequate overload and too frequently, you will short circuit both the recovery and growth processes.

OVERTRAINING AND CELLULAR DAMAGE

The clinical evidence that we need to train less frequently is finally starting to trickle in from the medical community. Research conducted by Michael Sherman back when he was a research associate at Ball State University in Indiana, strongly indicated that rest and recovery goes way beyond simply allowing ourselves to feel better, it's also absolutely essential to the cells of our bodies. In the January 1985 issue of American Health magazine, author Stephen Kiesling had this to say about Sherman's research: When Sherman aimed an electron microscope at the leg-muscle cells of marathon runners, he saw "twisted cells, torn cells, and cells turned inside out." And that was the day-before-the race damage from training. The day after the event, even more cells were battered.

In a related experiment, Sherman found that even after a full week of rest, marathon runners had not regained pre-race strength and power. Returning to moderate running after the marathon delayed recovery. And it may take months to recover from some races.[8]

While this study was performed on marathon runners who, admittedly, are the extreme example of high volume training, it could just as easily have been applied to bodybuilders with their twice a day, six to seven days per week, high volume and often ballistic training methods. According to Mentzer, bodybuilders may even be at greater risk owing to the higher over-loads with which they routinely train. According to him: "You've got to be real careful whenever you're training at peak overload levels. What I'm beginning to see much more clearly is just how demanding this stuff is. Arthur Jones said some years ago 'for every slight in-crease in intensity, there has to be a disproportionate decrease in volume,' and he wasn't joking."

"High intensity training places a demand on the body of an order that is phenomenal. If you were to draw a horizontal line, from left to right, across a sheet of paper with that line representing "0" effort then, off of that line, graph your daily effort output such as getting up in the morning, brushing your teeth, walking to your car, climbing some steps to get to work, etc., the graph representing that kind of effort output would barely leave the flat line. It would be a little squiggly sine wave. Then you go into the gym and perform a heavy set of partial bench presses. All of a sudden that little squiggly line would start to take off in a straight vertical line; off the paper, out the door, down the street and around the block! Within the space separating that peak of vertical ascent from the flat line is how much more biochemical resources have been used up. Do you see how dramatic a difference that is?" [9]

The conclusion to be drawn from both Mike Mentzer's and Michael Sherman's research is simply that overtraining is a very real problem and that the actual process of working out makes far greater systemic demands and creates far more cellular damage than was previously believed. Additionally, their work in conjunction with that of ours has revealed that it is also far easier to overtrain than was previously believed. Further, the recovery process, which always precedes the growth process, can take upwards of one full week to complete (or perhaps much longer) and training before the bi-phasic process of recovery and growth has taken place will only result in, at minimum, slower progress and, in the worst case, dangerous physical exhaustion.

STRESS AND ADAPTATION

The whole issue of recovery ability might be made more lucid if we looked at it in terms of the body's capacity to cope with stress. Up to a certain point, for example, exposure to the sun will lead to the formation of a tan. While our reason for tanning is a purely cosmetic one, the actual process of acquiring a tan is a perfect example of how our bodies adapt to protect our tissues from the stressor of ultraviolet light.

The adaptive process, whether in response to ultraviolet light or progressive overload weight training, is essentially defensive in nature. And the degree to which the process of adaptation is stimulated is directly proportional to the strength of the stressor. To follow through on our sun tanning example, if you decide to lay out in the sun in the middle of January, you can remain outside all day long and show little or no tan for your efforts. The reason is that the sun is not directly overhead at this time of year and, correspondingly, its rays are not as intense. The sun's rays must be of a certain strength in order to elicit an adaptive response from our bodies, i.e., the marshaling of the bodies store of melanin or skin pigment.

Conversely, when you decide to lay out in the hot sun in the middle of July, you don't have to wait hours, days, or weeks to see results, i.e., to stimulate an adaptive response. It's an immediate occurrence that is directly proportionate to the intensity or strength of the stressor (the sun directly overhead). Your skin gets red and slightly inflamed and the tanning process is almost instantaneous.

While it's beyond our immediate power to control the strength of the sun's rays, which are dependent upon the seasons, weight training happens to be a form of bodily stress over which we have direct control. The level of weight training overload is solely dependent upon our ability and willingness to generate the necessary effort required to overload our muscles.

Just as the sun is a form of stress to the skin, Precision Training is a form of stress to the muscles and the overall physical system. Heavy overload exercise, when not performed to excess, will stimulate a compensatory build-up in the form of added muscle tissue, which aids the body in coping more successfully with similar stressors in the future. Excessive exposure to the strong summer rays of the sun causes the skin to blister and "de-compensate" or break down. So, taken to extremes, as in the case of excessive sun, bodybuilders who insist on training six to seven days a week will witness a similar decompensatory effect. The resulting drain on the regulatory sub-systems of the body will actually prevent the build-up of muscle. All of the energy reserves will have to be utilized in an attempt to overcome the energy debt caused by the excessive overexposure to training.

SYMPTOMS OF OVERTRAINING

The trainee who has entered an overtrained state has many tell-tale symptoms of this condition. One of these is an almost constant sense of fatigue combined with a deep lack of energy and ambition. Chronic fatigue, according to Dr. Gabe Mirkin in The Sports Medicine Book, along with frequent colds and injuries are sure signs that you've overdone it. Mirkin lists these other signs as further indicators of overtraining:

- Persistent soreness and stiffness in the muscles, joints or tendons.

- Heavy-leggedness.

- Loss of interest in training.

- Nervousness.

- Depression — "I don't care" attitude.

- Inability to relax.

- A decrease in academic work or performance.

- Sleep problems.

- Headache.

- Loss of appetite.

- Fatigue and sluggishness.

- Loss of weight.

- Swelling of the lymph nodes in the neck, groin, and armpit.

- Constipation or diarrhea.

- In women, the absence of menstruation.

One of the more popular methods used to detect overtraining is to monitor the morning pulse rate. Upon arising, the athlete is instructed to take his pulse for 60 seconds. If it is seven beats a minute faster than usual, a layoff or reduction in training is indicated. Perhaps the most blatant symptom of overtraining is a very strong disinclination to train at all. Your body is signaling your brain that it hasn't fully recovered from the cumulative systemic toll of previous training sessions. Any person who falls into the habit of training five to six days a week over prolonged periods of time will inevitably become overtrained, regardless of how powerful or well built an individual may be.

Eventually, as you become stronger and are able to utilize even greater overload in your training sessions, you will find that even training three days per week will prove to be too much. At this point, it's recommended that you drop your weekly workouts to two, working half of the body in each one so that each body part gets trained once per week. As you again progress, you may need to decrease your training frequency to one workout per week and, later still, to one workout every two weeks.

Many bodybuilders who have been training for years never experience a state of overtraining and dismiss the notion as something that "can't happen" to them. In nine cases out of ten, the reason why they don't become overtrained is simply that they lack the drive to train with the requisite overload and effort to ever reach a condition of staleness. Plateaus are things that have to be progressed to, and henceforth from which all progress halts. And, in order to make progress, as we've seen, one must be willing to train with very high intensity which is something that these people, who don't make any perceptible progress from year to year, let alone from workout to workout, will never achieve.

HOW TO COMBAT OVERTRAINING

Now that we know what overtraining is, the question becomes: How do you get rid of the overtraining symptoms once you've acquired them? The problem is an individual one with each trainee obliged to consider his own case on its own merits. But some general or basic rules exist that apply to all human beings. First, it should be noted that there are varying degrees of overtraining.

For example, a bodybuilder can train for a month or two and make steady gains in both power and physique. Then all at once he'll cease progressing and, even though he eats plenty of nourishing foods, his body weight will not increase. He may have been driving himself to the limit in his training, striving to add a single repetition or a couple of pounds, yet failing continually to gain them.

There is only one thing to be done in a case like this and, fortunately, it works. What is it? Simply to take a short layoff from training. The lifter or bodybuilder not only needs freedom from his heavy overload routine, he also needs freedom from all of the mental stress that goes along with training; psyching for lifts, resolving to shatter personal bests, that sort of thing. In short, the trainee would do well to forget about training entirely and focus instead on attempting to cultivate a stress free mental environment of rest and sleep. He should try to get at least eight hours sleep a night, and try to get out into the fresh air as much as possible.

Stress-free pastimes such as companionship, movies

or reading books, and listening to music can help hasten the recovery from overtraining almost as much as the rest itself. Diet at this time should be high in proteins and carbohydrates. Fresh fruits, salads, vegetables, and certain dried fruits such as seedless raisins will all prove beneficial in this respect. A multiple vitamin-mineral supplement with extra "B" (the so-called "stress vitamin"), "C" and "E" vitamins can also help.

Most sensible weight trainers will take a lay-off as soon as they observe a stale period coming on. As a result, they're able to stave it off before it hits and prevent any further serious symptoms from developing. In many cases, three or four days of rest from training will work wonders and the trainee is soon ready to start back in again.

There are some trainees who, instead of resting, will try to train through their plateaus. They must remember that muscular soreness is not to be confused with overtraining. You can work soreness out of a muscle with a hard training session but you can't get rid of overtraining by engaging in more work. Just the reverse is true and the condition of overtraining becomes exacerbated by the trainees refusal to decrease his training. In severe cases, it can mean that the trainee will have to lay off for as long as three to six months simply to recover from the exhaustive systemic affects that have accumulated.

Fortunately, these cases are rare. When they do occur, a long rest from weight training is an absolute must. Not only is his body in a state of chronic fatigue, but the trainee's nervous system and adaptation energy are also in corresponding states of exhaustion and depletion. Continuing to force oneself to train for lengthy periods of time when a period of rest is needed will cause not only undue frustration and worry, but also, when carried to extremes, a catabolic condition owing to both the overwork and accumulated stress. There is no reason to reach this state using Precision Training as your guide. Your Power Factor and Power Index numbers will immediately indicate you are training too frequently by reflecting a steady decrease in magnitude.

There exist other factors to be considered in overtraining and it would certainly behoove the trainee to remember these important physiological points:

1. The greater the overload/intensity, the more rapid the approach of fatigue.

2. Depending on the force of output/work performed, if a sufficient rest interval is allowed between muscle contractions, i.e., rest between sets, no great fatigue is apparent.

3. Excessive outside stressors (non-workout induced) can hasten muscular fatigue and vice versa.

4. Marked fatigue in one group of muscles will diminish the capacity for work in other groups.

5. Fatigue is reduced faster by rest, wholesome food, correct schedules of exercise, sufficient sleep and proper stress management.

There is consolation to be found in the fact that layoffs are temporary and the time will soon come when weight training can be resumed. While you should always have enthusiasm for lifting in order to succeed, since enthusiasm is a large part of the trainee's success, it should be tempered somewhat because unbridled enthusiasm can quickly lead to excessive training (over training).

THE ABSOLUTE NECESSITY OF A TRAINING LOG BOOK

Because there are so many factors to be considered and so many variables encountered over the course of a training career, it's exceedingly difficult to mentally retain all of the knowledge that you have gathered from experience. It's doubtful there exists any arena of human endeavor where a person discovers the most direct route to

It is crucial to the proper application of Precision Training to keep track of your workouts.

his destination right at the outset. Most learning and ultimate achievements are reached through a process of trial and error. By making a trial and missing the mark then noting the error, you are in a position to make the necessary adjustments and, in so doing, move closer to your goal.

For this reason, it is crucial to the proper application of Precision Training to keep track of your workouts (frequency of exercise, exercises used, sets, reps, poundages and times) in order to have both an indicator of your progress and a plan for your next workout. According to Mike Mentzer, who kept a training log book throughout his entire competitive career, "becoming a massively developed bodybuilder takes time, a number of years in most cases. I do believe, however, that the amount of time it would take any person to develop to his fullest potential could be reduced dramatically if he were to keep a training journal from the day he began training."

If you view your training as a journey whose destination is the fulfillment of your physical potential, a training journal will serve as a sort of physiological road map. Keeping a proper record of every proper turn in addition to every mistake made along the way can help you avoid the pitfalls that will slow down your progress. A training log book serves as an historical record of your workouts, what recovery period yielded the best progress in between your workouts, and when a reduction in training volume and frequency should be indicated. It should also include your daily caloric intake (inclusive of the types of foods consumed). By recording your daily food consumption, you can calculate your nutritional requirements for future weight gain and loss as well as observe the effects of different diets on peak performance output.

Charting your progress can yield invaluable training data and, eventually, you'll have enough information in your training log book to make precise determinations on everything from overload volume to frequency of training for optimal results.

8

A PRECISION TRAINING NUTRITION SEMINAR

Although there exists no "magic" number of muscular pounds you will gain by following the Precision Training method, it is a safe bet that the minimum amount of pure muscle that an average male could expect to gain after one year of such training would be ten pounds. Although the material presented in this chapter is geared primarily toward gaining lean body mass, those who desire to lose weight or firm up will find the material contained herein of use as well. We mention the figure of ten pounds knowing full-well that some of you reading this book have the capacity to gain three to four times this amount over a 12 month period and could quite possibly gain ten pounds of lean muscle mass in as little as three workouts. Nevertheless, for the sake of illustration, let's assume that you are a reasonably advanced trainee and that you've struggled for years trying to increase your muscle mass stores and yet you still weigh the same, month after month, year after year, in spite of your efforts.

There are some exercise physiologists and experienced bodybuilders who believe that gaining even ten pounds of muscle a year would be a considerable achievement. Let it be understood right off the top that we're not referring here to simply gaining ten pounds of body weight — that's a relatively simple procedure — but rather ten pounds of pure muscle. On the surface, such an amount doesn't really sound like much to gain over a 12 month period. But looked at over the long term, say five years — which is how you have to look at a training career (nobody ever became Mr. Olympia in one year) — gaining at that rate of speed, in five years you would gain 50 pounds of muscle which is enough to transform the average adult male weighing 165 pounds into a 215 pound Mr. Olympia competitor.

Many Mr. Olympia competitors actually weigh much less than 215 pounds. These men are, whether they choose to admit to it or not, the thoroughbreds (genetically speaking) of our species. They are the reason the aforementioned exercise physiologists and bodybuilders ascertain the acquisition of ten pounds a year through training is almost beyond the reach of most of us lesser mortals.

But let's assume that we are all going to train hard enough to gain ten pounds of muscle this year. Granted we don't always think in terms of a year, or in blocks of five years. We think about daily progress, daily workouts and so forth. And, if you think that ten pounds of muscle growth in one year is slow, it's unbelievable how slow such growth computes on a daily level!

GAINING TEN POUNDS OF MUSCLE

If you divide ten pounds of muscle by the amount of days it took to gain it (365 days for one year), the number comes out to .027 pounds of muscle gained per day. This is the same as 12 grams, or less than half an ounce! That's not even enough to register on a body weight scale! Think for a moment just how minuscule 12 grams of muscle gain per day is — and that's assuming that you're gaining ten pounds of muscle per year! It's ridiculously slow. And yet, when we don't seem to be gaining fast enough the typical reaction is to increase our training time, increase our intake of supplements, and so forth. These things, however, don't hasten the muscle-growth process.

THE ROLE OF NUTRITION

Obviously gaining ten pounds of muscle (or more) is going to require some nutrition. At the very least, it's going to require enough nutrition to maintain health through what is referred to as a "well-balanced diet." But if you want to make sure that the weight you gain is all muscle, the question becomes how much food will you have to eat to gain these ten pounds of pure muscle without adding any fat? To answer this, you must first be made aware of the fact that one pound of muscle tissue contains 600 calories. This is true of all human beings whether I'm talking about you or Arnold Schwarzenegger.

If you were to surgically cut away a pound of muscle tissue, place it in a device known as a calorimeter, it would give off 600 calories of heat. It follows logically that, if one pound of muscular mass contains 600 calories and you wanted to gain ten pounds, then you would have to consume 600 × 10, or 6,000, calories a year over and above your maintenance need of calories. That's 6,000 extra calories a year. Not 6,000 extra calories a day.

Bodybuilders, being what they are, don't tend to think in terms of a year because there exists a pervasive attitude that things have to happen in terms of days! They want to know how many extra calories they need on a daily basis. Well, to obtain this answer it's again a pretty elementary exercise in mathematics. Divide those 6,000 calories by 365 (the number of days there are in a year), and you come out with the answer that you need approximately 16 extra calories a day over and above your maintenance need of calories to grow ten pounds of muscle a year. You're not going to grow those ten pounds of muscle a year, however, simply by eating 16 extra calories a day over and above your maintenance need of calories. The process of eating, in itself, actually contributes nothing to the growth process.

THE FIRST REQUISITE OF MUSCLE GROWTH

The first requisite for muscle growth is that you've got to stimulate your muscles to grow through your training. Then, and only then, does nutrition play a role.

You have to provide adequate nutrition to maintain your existing physical mass then you've got to provide that tiny bit of extra nutrition to allow for that tiny bit of extra growth that might be taking place on a daily basis. And we say "might be taking place," because it will all depend on how successful your efforts were in the gym. Again, keep in mind how minuscule growth is on a daily basis to gain ten pounds of muscle a year.

GETTING ENOUGH CALORIES FOR GROWTH TO TAKE PLACE

For practical purposes, the majority of trainees already eat more than necessary to grow ten pounds of muscle a year. That's why so few of us have ultra low body fat, i.e., are "ripped." Most of us are actually eating too many calories. If you're not growing muscular mass now, and you're eating sufficiently, what's the reason you're not growing? Answer: You're not stimulating growth in your training sessions. In short, you're not training with sufficient progressive muscular overload. Incidentally, very rarely is the answer to a muscular growth problem nutritional, particularly in North America, because most everybody eats more than adequately. We're not suggesting that you count your calories this precisely every day to make sure that you grow just muscular mass. What we're trying to point out by doing this arithmetic is that you don't have to force feed yourself hundreds or even thousands of extra calories a day, or hundreds of extra grams of protein with the mistaken notion that, in so doing, you'll hasten the muscle-growth process.

DETERMINING YOUR "MAINTENANCE" NEED OF CALORIES

We've mentioned that to allow for ten pounds of muscle growth to manifest itself over the course of a year you have to consume an additional 6,000 calories over and above your maintenance need of calories, given, of course, that you stimulated that growth in the first place. Granted, there is a certain metabolic "cost" in the growth process, which may bump that extra caloric intake number to 17 or 18 calories a day. Obviously, all of this is oversimplified but nevertheless it serves to give you some idea of just how slow the muscle-growth process can be and how little additional supplementation or nutrition you really need to allow muscular growth to manifest. There exists a certain, specific amount of calories you require every day that maintains your present body weight, i.e., you don't gain weight and you don't lose weight at this number. This is referred to as your "maintenance" need of calories. Then, to grow an additional ten pounds of muscle a year, you have to tack on an extra 16 calories above that number on a daily basis. This simple procedure is, in essence, the nutritional "secret" to gaining muscular weight.

One way to discover your daily caloric need is to multiply your present body weight by ten then add the resulting integer to twice your body weight. This is a fairly accurate "rule of thumb" to determine one's maintenance need of calories, but perhaps the simplest way is to write down every single thing you eat, from the milk and sugar you put in your coffee to the dressing you put on your salads, over a random five day period. Then, after each day is over, sit down with a calorie counting book and calculate your total number of calories for that day. At the end of the five day period, take your five total numbers, add them up, and divide this number by five. The resulting sum will be your daily average maintenance need of calories.

For example: Monday: You consume 2500 calories. Tuesday: You consume 2700 calories. Wednesday: It's the middle of the week, you're getting tired and frustrated from your job, you pig out and have 4500 calories. Thursday: You feel guilty and decide to atone for your dietary aberrations by only having 1500 calories. Friday: You're back to normal and you reach your daily average of around 2500 calories.

Now take these five numbers and add them up (2,500 + 2,700 + 4,500 + 1,500 + 2,500 = 13,700 calories). Then divide this number by the number of days involved (five) and your resulting number of 2,740 calories is your daily average calorie intake. Now, if over this five day period you haven't gained weight or lost weight, it's your daily maintenance need of calories. This is the precise amount of calories you need to maintain your present body weight.

This procedure, incidentally, takes into account your individual Basal Metabolic Rate (BMR) and your voluntary physical activity output. It doesn't even matter how fast or slow your metabolism is — it's all taken into account with this method. While your BMR is unique, (that is, it's different for everybody), it's still factored into this method of determining your daily need of calories.

It's important (for obvious reasons) that you don't change your diet during this period; you want to find out what your daily maintenance need of calories is. Then, if you want to gain ten pounds of muscle a year, you tack on 16 calories and you consume a grand total of 2,756 by this example. Sixteen extra calories a day can be gotten by taking two bites out of an apple. And again, how many bodybuilders do you know who force-feed themselves hundreds or even thousands of extra calories a day with the mistaken notion they're hastening the muscle-growth process? It's almost a too simplistic logic that if you eat more you're going to grow faster. That's true but what you'll be growing is fat.

HOW MUCH PROTEIN DO YOU NEED?

A lot of bodybuilders seem preoccupied with protein and how much extra protein is required to build muscle. Well, if we look again to our hypothetical example of growing ten pounds of muscle a year, we see that it requires roughly 16 calories a day over and above our maintenance need of calories. As cited before, muscle tissue is comprised of approximately 25% protein. It's actually 22%, but for the sake of argument, let's assume that muscle tissue is comprised of 25% protein.

Out of those 16 calories, about four of those calories (25%) should be protein calories. It just so happens that one gram of protein contains four calories, so to grow ten pounds of muscle a year we need to consume one gram of protein beyond our maintenance need of protein every day. There do exist those faddists who honestly believe that if they don't have their hourly protein drink, their strength will decrease 50 pounds — and it does, because they believe it. This power of suggestion is called the "placebo effect."

■ BUT AREN'T SOME PROTEINS MORE "ANABOLIC" THAN OTHERS?

No. All proteins are broken down into the same essential elements: amino acids, glucose, fatty acids, etc. In order to be used by the human body they're all broken down into exactly the same thing.

■ BUT AREN'T LARGE AMOUNTS OF PROTEIN FOODS AND SUPPLEMENTS NECESSARY TO BUILD BIG MUSCLES?

Contrary to much of what you've probably read, most of us in North America already get more than enough protein from our diets. You would have to look long and hard to find many trainees who are actually deficient in this macro nutrient.

You must understand that protein is not utilized to fuel your workouts. Individual protein requirements are dependent solely upon individual body weight. Under normal circumstances, protein is not a fuel source. Consequently, daily need for this macro nutrient is not contingent upon how active you are in the gym. McMaster University, one of Canada's leading exercise and nutrition-science centers, recently released studies indicating that bodybuilders, who often consume up to three and four times the recommended daily intake of protein, actually need only 10% extra protein per day.

According to the studies, joggers who log more than 100 kilometers (60 miles) a week need more protein than bodybuilders. Cells and tissue, particularly muscle, are based on proteins which are also an energy source. But our bodybuilding workouts are fueled solely by glucose derived from carbohydrates (barring a starvation diet) so these proteins are "spared" for their primary purpose of tissue growth and repair.

Although the body's requirements rise under certain conditions such as pregnancy or when body weight is elevated, most people throughout North America and Europe inadvertently ingest more protein than they need. There is also evidence that consuming large quantities of protein may actually cause damage to the kidneys and liver. The metabolism and excretion of these non-storable protein loads imposes major stress and can cause excessive growth of these vital organs. The researchers at McMaster University calculated daily protein requirements by monitoring intake and output of protein in the subjects' sweat, urine, and feces (and you thought a physiologist's work was all glamour and lecture circuits!). The recommended average daily intake for adults is 0.7 grams of protein per kilogram of body weight. For a 154-pound bodybuilder, this translates to about 49 grams of protein a day. This is the equivalent of 16 ounces of milk, three ounces of chicken, five slices of bread, or four cups of spaghetti. We can hear the cries of protest already: "But this figure of .7 is based on what the average individual requires, and bodybuilders work much harder than the average individual." Fine. So let's boost that percentage by 28.5% to .9 grams of protein per kilogram of body weight (remember that bodybuilders may be more active than the average man — but not that much more active and that the requirements are body weight dependent as opposed to activity level dependent). That same 154-pound bodybuilder now needs 63 grams of protein a day — only 14 more grams!

The following formula can be used to determine your specific protein requirements:

1. Divide your weight in pounds by 2.2 then round off the resulting integer to the nearest whole number.

2. Multiply this number by .9

3. The number you're left with will be your specific daily protein requirement in grams. It should be noted, however, that each time your body weight increases or decreases, you must recalculate your protein requirements. Failure to do so could upset your bodybuilding progress. Protein consumed in excess of the body's

needs is either excreted from the body, which represents a waste of money, or worse, stored as fat, which represents, well, ...fat.

THE FUEL OF PRECISION TRAINING IS SUGAR

Precision Training, or any other form of weight training for that matter, doesn't burn all that many calories. And the calories that it does burn are sugar calories. It doesn't matter how you train; whether it's Precision Training or any other system. Any kind of weight training is considered a high intensity activity, and all high intensity activities depend entirely upon glucose as fuel. So, if you're trying to lose weight, or lose fat to get cut up, weight training is the worst way to do it. Weight training uses 90% glucose for fuel whereas aerobic activity will use up to 80 or 90% fat as fuel. If you're looking to get cut up, use Precision Training to either build or maintain your muscle mass then spend as much of the rest of the time you have doing aerobic activities to burn fat. This is not an opinion, it's a fact that can be backed up by any exercise physiologist or medical doctor.

THE BEST DIET TO FOLLOW IN ORDER TO BUILD MASS

Simply eat a well-balanced diet. The most important aspect of eating a well-balanced diet is that it maintain health. This is something we all learned in eighth grade health class. It also happens to be something that we often forget, that the first requisite in building a strong healthy body is maintaining health, and the best way to maintain health is to eat a well-balanced diet.

A well-balanced diet is one that is comprised of 60%

carbohydrates, 25% protein and 15% fats. That means if your daily maintenance need of calories is 3,000, out of those 3,000 calories, 60% should be carbohydrates, 25% protein and 15% fats. According to nutritional scientists and physical educators, a well-balanced diet is comprised of 60% carbohydrates, 25% protein and 15% fat. You will find quacks and faddists who say eat the majority of your calories from protein. In most instances those people sell protein and have a vested interest in distorting nutritional reality.

THE SUPREME IMPORTANCE OF CARBOHYDRATES

Carbohydrates, next to water, are by far the most important nutritional element anybody, not just body-builders, could consume. The most important reason being our nervous systems, our brains, our spinal cords, our peripheral nerves, derive 99.9% of their nutrition from the one thing that we've been taught is the worst thing we could eat: Sugar. Glucose — it's the most important thing you could eat — pure simple sugar. Your brain derives 99% of its nutrition from sugar.

People who go on low-carbohydrate diets will notice a pronounced lack of energy almost immediately. They will feel weak, tense, edgy, and suffer impairment of concentration and short-term memory; they will start dreaming about chocolate instead of sex. What are these signals? It is their nervous systems sending out for the one thing they need most — sugar! If you've ever been around a bodybuilder who has been on a low-carb diet for six weeks or so, you would have seen it impair his personality. Your personality is a product of your nervous system and, if your nervous system is not getting the fuel it needs from carbohydrates, your personality is going to become altered. I've seen body-builders do weird things and I've often wondered if their behavior was the result of being on a low carbohydrate diet too long. Anybody who has been around bodybuilding for a long time behind the scenes knows that a lot of bodybuilders can seem crazy. They do strange things and I think it's because of the one-time voguish low carbohydrate diet; it affects the thinking process and it affects personality. Low blood sugar will definitely cause an erratic behavior. It's in all of the medical journals.

■ WHAT ABOUT "SIMPLE" AND "COMPLEX" CARBOHYDRATES?

There is no such thing as simple or complex carbo-hydrates. A carbohydrate is a carbohydrate. There are simple and complex, or refined and unrefined foods, but the carbohydrate has to be in the form of glucose by the time it gets into your bloodstream.

It makes no difference at all whether it's from a candy bar, an apple, or a baked potato, it has to be in the form of glucose for your brain to use it. "Refined" and "unrefined" refers to the prepared condition of the food it's contained in. The carbohydrate is the same. It isn't a good practice to eat too many refined sugars or simple sugars though, because they get into your blood-stream too fast and cause all kinds of problems. It's preferable to get your carbohydrates from as many natural sources as possible but, if you have a hankering to have an occasional candy bar, don't think the world's going to stop revolving if you eat it. The reason nutri-tional experts advocate that you try to get your carbo-hydrates from fruits and vegetables is because those foods contain vitamins and minerals along with other nutrients essential to a well-balanced diet.

■ HOW DO I KNOW IF MY DIET IS WELL-BALANCED?

Very simple. If there's one issue in bodybuilding that has been confused, it is that of nutrition. Good nutrition is really not complicated. It may seem over simplistic but all you have to do is eat a simple well-balanced diet, which is really nothing more than consuming products from what used to be called the four basic food groups. The four basic food groups are:

1. fruits & vegetables
2. cereals & grains
3. dairy products
4. meat

If you're getting two portions every day from each of these categories, you will be consuming a well-balanced diet. Even simpler, if you eat a little bit of everything but not too much of anything you'll be getting a well-balanced diet. The matter of diet is really very simple. Complicating the matter and confusing it are some of the crazy articles you read in some of the muscle magazines which are designed solely to sell you more products by confusing you and muddying the issue. By doing so they're able to divest you of your hard-earned dollars much easier.

THE ROLE OF SUPPLEMENTS

The question invariably comes up "Where do supplements fit in?" Well, if you're eating a well-balanced diet then, theoretically, you don't need supplements because a well-balanced diet is just that; a well-balanced diet. By definition, you're getting everything you need, all the vitamins, minerals, carbohydrates, proteins, fats and water you need to maintain health. It's often not possible to get a well-balanced diet, however, due to time pressures, family pressures, job pressures, etc. We have to skip meals from time to time. If you suspect that you're not getting a well-balanced diet, then by all means, include an all-round vitamin-mineral tablet or protein supplement.

There exists no need whatsoever to spend hundreds of dollars a month on useless vitamins and minerals that you're just going to pass through your system anyway. And you can see it. For instance, taking too much Vitamin B will turn your urine bright yellow. Take supplements only when you think you may not be getting a well-balanced diet, such as before a contest while you're on a low calorie diet because, once your calorie intake reaches a certain low level, you can't get a well-balanced diet. Some nutritional scientists say that once you go below 1500 calories it's impossible to get all the vitamins, proteins, and minerals you need to maintain proper health and, of course, build a big muscular physique.

■ WHAT IS THE MOST EFFICIENT FUEL FOR BODYBUILDING PURPOSES?

In a word, carbohydrates. Carbohydrates are the most efficient fuel for Precision Training or any kind of anaerobic training. Anaerobic activity (weight training) demands sugar for fuel. The worst way to get defined muscularity, by the way. is to lift weights. Weight lifting does not burn fat for fuel. It's a simple medical fact not open to debate; weight lifting burns sugar and if you're not getting sugar from dietary carbohydrates like fruits, vegetables, cereals or grains, where is your muscle going to get the sugar it requires for high-intensity contractions? Where is your body going to get the necessary sugar to continue contracting? Answer: From your own muscle tissue! There's an amino acid contained in your muscle tissue called alanine, which will be broken down in your liver and turned into glucose. That's why carbohydrates are called "protein sparing," it spares your protein from being used for energy.

You can always tell when you start using muscle for energy. We pointed out earlier that one pound of muscle tissue contains 600 calories while one pound of fat contains 3500 calories. If you were to start burning muscle for energy, how many pounds of muscle would you have to burn in order to get the same energy yield from one pound of fat? Almost six pounds! You will know when you start using muscle for energy because you will start losing weight rapidly — very rapidly — like two to five pounds a day. Look at the disparity here; 600 calories vs. 3500 calories. To get the same energy yield from muscle that you would from fat you would have to burn 6 pounds of muscle. It's ridiculous to go on low carbohydrate diets to get defined muscles because you will, inevitably, lose some muscle. The best way to get cut up is go on a reduced calorie diet by reducing your daily calorie intake to below your daily maintenance need of calories. Again, if you need 3,000 calories a day to maintain your existing body weight and, all of a sudden, you reduce your daily calorie intake to 2,000 calories, then you're going to be 1,000 calories deficient. Where are those 1,000 calories going to come from? Your body fat. That's what body fat is; stored energy.

■ SHOULD I JUST EAT PROTEIN FOODS WHEN I'M DIETING TO GET DEFINED?

No. It's ridiculous to attempt muscle definition by eating nothing but protein, or tuna fish and water as some bodybuilders do. Not only is it unpleasant and unhealthy, it's highly counterproductive. Any time you have to diet drastically to lose body fat you will invariably lose some muscle mass. It's better to try to build muscle and stay lean throughout the year then zero-in six to eight weeks before each contest. Get the body fat off then eat a maintenance allotment of calories to stay at roughly 6% body fat all year.

WHY YOU SHOULD STAY LEAN

If you look at a bodybuilder who goes on a "zero carbohydrate diet" for a contest, you'll notice a very common phenomenon that happens immediately afterward — he gets fat. It's inevitable because of the body's protective mechanism. The body doesn't want to lose all of its body fat. As far as the body is concerned it's starving, it's dying. And it's going to protect itself against this "famine" in the future by putting on as much fat as possible. The best thing to do if you desire to stay defined year-round is to get lean slowly over a period of time then sanely maintain that lower body fat level by eating a well-balanced diet.

■ FAT ADDS NOTHING

Contrary to what some would have you believe, fat adds nothing in the way of an advantage to body strength. Instead, it hinders body strength. It has been discovered that intramuscular fat (fat in between muscle fibers) actually hinders contraction which serves to make you weaker. The leaner you are, the stronger you'll be. You should stay lean as much of the time as possible.

Section Two
ADVANCED PRECISION TRAINING

9

MAXIMUM OVERLOAD FOR MAXIMUM GAINS

There exists a direct correlation between how much overload you can impose on a muscle and how much size and strength it can acquire. The greater the overload imposed, the greater the potential size and strength increase. Specific demands imposed upon the body result in specific physiological adjustments. This fact forms a concept central to exercise physiology known as the principle of Specific Adaptation to Imposed Demands (SAID). That is, if training is to be performed for the purpose of stimulating increases in strength and size, then the demands must be of a specific nature — namely peak overload and maximum muscular output. But as our bodies adapt to a certain level of resistance by developing larger and stronger muscles, the overload in our workouts must be increased if further growth is to be achieved. This cause and effect relationship has been labeled the Progressive Overload Principle which states that in order to grow progressively larger muscles the skeletal muscles must be routinely subjected to ever-increasing demands. This is not only one of the most basic principles of strength development, it's also the cornerstone of Precision Training.

THE LAW OF MUSCLE FIBER RECRUITMENT

The sole objective, as far as building muscular mass is concerned, is muscle fiber recruitment. The more muscle fibers recruited, the more activated, and the more activated, the greater the growth stimulation. Therefore, it stands to reason that the more muscle fibers called into play or made to contract against resistance, the more muscle fibers will be stimulated to hypertrophy or grow larger. It was demonstrated clinically in 1973 that, at light loads, slow-twitch fibers contract and are capable of sustaining repeated contractions at this relatively low intensity. Since these fibers are weaker, they are not suited to a higher intensity of effort or overload. If a greater load is imposed upon the muscle, a progressive recruitment of larger and stronger (fast-twitch) muscle fibers occurs. Thus, when the load increases from light to heavy there is a progressive increase in the number and type of muscle fibers involved in the contraction. Light loads, regardless of how many sets and reps you perform with them, recruit primarily slow-twitch muscle fibers which have the lowest capacity to increase in size. Heavier loads, on the other hand, recruit fast-twitch fibers in addition to the slow-twitch fibers already activated. From this we can conclude that the amount of weight lifted, as opposed to the speed of the contraction, is what recruits and stimulates the greatest amount of muscle fibers, thereby allowing for the greatest increases in size and strength.[10]

As a result, you must consistently strive to lift heavier and heavier weights if you expect to increase your Power Factor. Consistent increases in size and strength are your goals, after all, and if you have the fiber recruitment potential to bench press 200 pounds for six sets of 30 repetitions, and yet the most you ever lift in any given workout is 125 pounds for six sets of 30 repetitions, then neither your muscle mass nor your strength will ever increase. They don't have to, as the muscles are only being called upon to do work that's well below their existing maximum capacity. Work, incidentally, completely capable of being handled solely by the slow twitch fibers which happen to be the ones having the least growth potential.

HOW SIZE AND POWER ARE CREATED

What is the relationship between how a muscle grows and why a muscle grows? Please note that these are two very distinct issues, the answers to which are found in two distinct physiological processes. Muscle grows through a process of overcompensation in direct proportion to the overload it has to contract against. The greater the overload imposed on the muscle, the greater the growth stimulation and, of course, the over-compensation (muscle mass increase).

Why muscle grows is because the body's muscular status quo (homeostasis) has been threatened via suffi-cient overload having been placed upon it, and because sufficient time has elapsed since that overload was im-posed to allow the body's recuperative subsystems time to do two things: 1) recover from the stressor of training and 2) overcompensate or enlarge upon its existing muscle mass stores to prevent a similar stressor from disrupting the body to the same extent the next time.

The acquisition of inordinate levels of power and muscle mass cannot be brought about by gently coaxing or cajoling the muscles nor by the popular, though erroneous, notion of "confusing" them. Instead, they must be made to work to the limit of their uppermost capabilities for as long as possible, which is not really very long at all for the vast majority, even though individual variations may exist. Muscle growth is a systemic response to a tremendous overload having been imposed on the muscles via their contracting, whether concentrically, statically, eccentrically or in combination, against a very heavy and demanding resistance (high Power Factor). If an individual is willing to exert himself maximally, and the resistance utilized in his workouts is of a progressive nature, an increase will occur in the size and strength of his skeletal muscles.

MUSCLE GROWTH AS SYSTEMIC, NOT LOCALIZED

Much of the confusion that has arisen in the realm of strength training has resulted from the belief that the muscle-growth process is a phenomenon of a localized nature rather than systemic. This notion is erroneous, however, as it is the Central Nervous System (CNS) that triggers the growth process, a process which cannot be called into play by the isolated and protracted performance of highly repetitive tasks that are of a level well within the body's existing muscular capacity.

Growth is systemic and the "trigger" mechanism signaling the body to grow can only be turned on by a "call to arms" from the Central Nervous System.

Growth isn't easy. It must literally be forced. Such being the case, how does one force growth with light weights or mild exertion? The answer is one can't — at least, not without steroids and growth drugs.

RESEARCH ON REPETITION VARIATIONS

A heavy weight lifted as many times as possible within a given unit of time imposes a maximum overload, not only on the localized muscles but, more importantly, on the CNS, and this is the most important requirement for developing larger and stronger muscles. The Power Index, however, can actually decrease if the resistance is so heavy that only one or two repetitions are possible as the actual muscular output, i.e., pounds lifted per minute, falls way off, thereby diminishing muscular overload.

Further, scientific research conducted by S. Grillner and M. Udo, indicated that while parallel increases in load and muscle fiber recruitment occur, this process happens only up to a certain threshold point they perceived to be at 50% of a muscle's maximum voluntary contractile ability. Their research indicated that 90% of all available muscle fibers in a targeted muscle group have been activated with a load that is roughly 50% of a muscle's one rep maximum.[11]

In other words, the weight selected for training should be heavy enough to recruit most of the available muscle fibers: slow, intermediate and fast twitch. But once this threshold is reached, going heavier will not necessarily recruit more muscle fibers and can, depending upon innate fiber type distribution, actually diminish muscular output, i.e., your Power Factor.

ALTERATIONS IN NERVE DISCHARGE

It would appear that gains obtained in strength from a program utilizing weights that are in the 90-100% range of a subject's one rep maximum weight for low repetitions (1-6) are not necessarily the result of a still greater degree of fiber recruitment but more the result of alterations in the pattern of nerve discharge. Research by H.S. Milner-Brown and colleagues strongly corroborated this notion and went on to reveal that the discharge of impulses appear to synchronize in response to muscular contraction against resistances close to 100% of a muscle's maximum voluntary contractile ability.[12]

Evidently what happens in this respect is that the synchronization parlays into better timing between the nerves innervating the muscle and the rate of contraction. This results in the impulses for muscular contraction occurring more or less simultaneously, heightening the electrical input into the muscle at one time and significantly amplifing the contractile force capacity of the existing fibers irrespective of their actual size.

Therefore, lifting a weight that is over 50% but under 100% of a trainee's one rep maximum weight for as many repetitions as possible will produce the best results. This broad repetition variation must exist owing to such diverse innate physiological conditions as predominant fiber type, neuromuscular contractile efficiency, age and sex, as well as numerous other considerations among individuals. The heavy weights will ensure that all available muscle fibers (slow, intermediate and fast twitch) will have been activated while the higher repetitions will lead to greater muscular output on a pounds per minute basis (overload) resulting in the highest possible Power Index and greater muscle growth stimulation. All of this efficiency occurs maximally at the "sweet spot" referred to in Chapter 3 where the weight on the bar and the number of corresponding reps generate your maximum Power Factor.

COMPETITIVE WEIGHTLIFTERS NEED HEAVIER WEIGHTS

For those more interested in the development of strength, qua strength, it would obviously be of benefit to train with weights closer to 100% of their one rep maximum and, per force, lower repetitions, as so doing would improve their neural activity, hence, their chances for competitive success. This has been corroborated by research conducted by D.H. Clarke which indicated that such a systemic response to training can be elicited only when trainees employed weights approaching 90-100% of their one rep maximums for sets of 1-6 repetitions.[13]

Anything less than this percentage would compromise their objectives of stimulating maximum strength increases. There would exist no need to improve upon or alter the existing patterns of nerve discharge within particular muscle groups during the performance of specific competitive lifts.

THE BOTTOM LINE

It's important to keep in mind with all of the conclusions that have been predicated upon the percentage of one rep maximum research, that, owing to the immense range of genetic variability among individuals, a one size fits all repetition prescription is not only impractical but speculative at best. The bottom line is muscular output or overload. As long as an individual's Power Factor and Power Index are consistently increasing the trainee is doing all that he reasonably can to stimulate maximum increases in his size and strength.

WHY MULTIPLE EXERCISES ARE NOT NECESSARY

Many bodybuilders have adopted the age-old contention that a variety of exercises for a particular muscle "must" be performed in order to activate all of a given muscle's fibers. But, as we've just learned, the law of muscle fiber recruitment renders this belief invalid. It's the force required to lift a weight that determines and activates the amount of fibers recruited and not the number of exercises performed. Choosing light weight, multiple exercises is both inefficient and ineffective.

TRAINING FOR "SHAPE"

There is also the popular, though erroneous, belief (it exists in many training circles) that by varying the angle at which a muscle is trained, the trainee will, somehow, be able to direct the stress imposed to specific areas of a muscle and can thereby "shape" the muscle being trained. This is a belief that has absolutely no basis in fact. The reason is the way a muscle is innervated. The nerves that enter a given muscle divide out into threads that resemble branches on a tree. Each branch ends at the muscle cell and carries the electrochemical current that causes each muscle cell to contract.[14]

When this current is released, all of the cells serviced by the branch (a single neuron) contract simultaneously (the "all or none" law of muscle fiber contraction), not some at the exclusion of others. It is simply not possible to isolate one portion, border, or ridge of a muscle. According to Dr. Fred Hatfield in his book, Bodybuilding: A Scientific Approach, the cells associated with each motor unit are spread all through the gross muscle, all portions of the gross muscle are affected similarly by a given exercise and therefore develop similarly. This is called the Principle of Noncontiguous Innervation. Using many variations of an exercise for one muscle in no way ensures more growth or different growth patterning than does performing the basic exercise...The shape of that muscle will not be affected by variations in the angle or position of stress application. Does this mean that all a bodybuilder has to do is perform the basic movement, and rid himself or herself of the array of supplemental exercises for a given muscle? I suspect it does.[15] Muscle shape is a function of genetics, that's why the "muscle shaping" advocates can't perform an exercise to make a biceps muscle look like a triangle, a hexagon or Mount Rushmore.

OTHER ELEMENTS OF PRODUCTIVE EXERCISE

As important as it is to lift progressively heavier and heavier weights to stimulate continuous increases in size and strength, it's not the only factor. Contraction is of equal importance. To induce maximum levels of muscle growth, as many of a muscle's fibers as possible must be made to contract simultaneously. The law of muscle fiber recruitment makes it abundantly clear that you must use a load of at least a threshold poundage. It is known that, in the body's ongoing effort to conserve energy, only the minimum number of muscle fibers required to perform a particular movement will be activated for any given demand.

THE ROLE OF SUPPLY AND DEMAND

The relationship between muscular stimulation and growth is one of supply and demand and, for muscle growth to be supplied, there must first be a very serious demand for it. After all, the primary concern of all living organisms is the acquisition and preservation of energy in order to better preserve the maintenance of the body's internal status quo, known as "homeostasis." The growth of muscle tissue beyond normal levels is a disruption of this status quo and requires additional energy for building and maintenance. Muscles will grow only when there is a tremendous physiological demand for them to do so. If a muscle's existing level of size and strength is adequate for handling workloads normally encountered (normal Power Factors), there will be no growth because there is no need for it.

The growth of muscle tissue then, is a process that must be literally forced to take place. What is important to keep in mind is the fact that the human body will do everything it possibly can to maintain its existing condition. It will not waste precious resources building a larger musculature than it perceives to be necessary. It's up to you to give your body a reason to grow progressively larger and stronger muscles and this can only be accomplished through maximum muscular output training with heavy weights. Precision Training, utilizing the advanced technique of strongest-range repetitions, has shown to deliver the greatest possible amount of overload to a working muscle. This, in turn, stimulates the body's overcompensation mechanism into action and results very quickly in maximal increases in the size and strength of its muscle tissue.

A STRONGER MUSCLE IS A BIGGER MUSCLE

It's a physiological fact that a muscle's strength is directly proportional to its cross-sectional area. In other words, if you want to get bigger, you've got to get stronger, and vice versa. The major physiological response to overload training is an increase in muscle fiber size. Trained muscle fibers tend to be larger than untrained muscle fibers. There are actually a variety of factors, however, that affect muscle strength and muscle size. The type and density of muscle fibers, the location of tendon insertions, and the length of muscle bellies are inherited characteristics that cannot be altered through training. Consequently, some people posses a greater genetic potential for developing muscle size and strength.

It isn't always possible to assess muscle strength solely by external measurements, however, because greater muscle strength is accompanied by greater muscle weight. Body composition evaluations provide a better means for determining changes in an individual's muscle mass. Although not everyone can develop huge muscles, everyone can increase muscle density and strength through Precision Training.

10

STRONGEST-RANGE TRAINING: THE HIGHEST RUNG ON THE LADDER

Precision Training is the only weight training system that provides you with an objective measurement of the overload that you are generating during an exercise. Further, since this overload must be progressive, there will come a point when you will be unable to increase the overload due to having reached the limits of your strength. There is a very powerful technique, however, which permits you to continue to increase the overload by avoiding the very factor that limits its progression. Simply put; avoid your weak range of motion. This is done by limiting the range of motion in each exercise to the strongest-range only.

To attain a maximum overload requires exercises that allow the muscles of the body to be worked in their strongest possible range of motion, using what you would now consider to be unbelievably heavy weights. This is the theory behind strongest-range or maximum overload training.

Take the bench press as an example. The weakest range of motion in the bench press is when you first move the weight up a few inches from your chest. The strongest-range of motion is during the last few inches of your reach. The authors personally supervised the workouts of a subject whose maximum workout weight on the bench press was 200 pounds. He was limited to this weight because it was the most he could handle while training in his weakest range. It was quickly discerned, however, that his muscles were capable of handling much more resistance than he had been providing to them. He was, in fact, capable of using 365 pounds for repetitions, but because his mind was locked into the notion that he had to perform full-range reps ("to develop the full muscle"), only the amount of fibers required to move 200 pounds were ever called into play. Once he started training with the maximum weight that his muscles were capable of lifting in his strongest range, his size and strength grew on a very consistent basis. The contention that he required a full-range of motion in order to build "full" or the entire breadth and length of his muscles has been proven erroneous owing to innervation, the fiber recruitment process, and the nature of overload training. All academics aside, it simply stands to reason that training to failure in your strongest-range of motion is a lot more intense and demanding than training to failure in your weakest range of motion. Since the weights utilized are greater, more muscle fibers are required and activated to move them. Further, the recovery period following such a workout must also be greater. Why? Because the greater weights, combined with the greater muscular output required to move them, results in a greater depth of systemic fatigue.

The concept of strongest-range training was a principle element in our first book, Power Factor Training. The success of this technique has now been corroborated by thousands of athletes from around the world, evidenced by the many letters and phone calls we have received from trainees who testify to its effectiveness.

To attain a maximum overload requires exercises that allow the muscles of the body to be worked in their strongest possible range of motion, using what you would now consider to be unbelievably heavy weights.

SPECIFICITY OF TRAINING

Specific training methods result in specific training effects. In physiology circles, this is known as the principle of Specific Adaptation to Imposed Demands, or SAID, and is among the most fundamental to a proper understanding of the cause and effect relationship between exercise and muscle growth. More will be said of this important physiological principle later in this book but for now, suffice it to say that, when you train specifically for size and strength, i.e., training in your strongest-range of motion, the results will come rapidly in as much as they'll be in proportion to the overload you impose on your muscles and their corresponding output. Conversely, if you train non-specifically (with full-range movements), the neuromuscular training stimulus is divided at least two different ways:

1. Size and strength.
2. Flexibility.

The effect is that your potential size and strength results, so fundamentally important to bodybuilders and strength athletes, are at least half of what they could be.

Full-range of motion is not a requirement for over-loading a muscle and overload is the only systemic stimulus that results in muscle growth. Granted, there is overload provided by fullrange movements, but, just as assuredly, that overload is not anywhere near what it has the potential to be as evidenced by the reduced poundages you're restricted to utilizing. Admittedly, some individuals can use some phenomenal poundages for full-range reps, but this shows only that these train-ees have a tremendously strong weak range of motion. Certainly much stronger than the average trainee. It also stands to reason that, if their weak range of motion is quite strong, their strongest-range of motion, by definition, would be even stronger and, hence, capable of recruiting and stimulating even more muscle fibers, thereby increasing their muscle growth potential.

Insofar as strength athletes and weight lifters of re-nown are concerned, there have been many who have used the technique of strongest-range repetitions. Physical fitness and bodybuilding pioneer, Joe Weider, wrote extensively about the technique back in the 1940s which caused many individuals to experiment but few, if any, of his readers fully recognized the signi-ficance of the technique's potential. Nevertheless, all admitted that they knew they were on to something when they employed the technique. Consider the fol-lowing:

1. The famed Olympic weight lifting gold medalist (1956), the late Paul Anderson, hit upon the method of performing partial repetitions early in his career and became a world champion before the age of 21. His back lift of 6,270 pounds still stands some 38 years later, according to the Guinness Book of World Records, as "the greatest weight ever lifted by a human being." Anderson was one of the pioneers in the field of partials, having made an indepth study of the technique's effectiveness by incorporating it into his own workouts. Because Power racks and Smith Machines did not exist in Anderson's time, the mighty native of Toccoa, Georgia would perform his partials by suspending massively loaded barbells from chains hanging off the branches of trees in his back yard. These weights would be lowered to a point that was roughly four inches above his head and Anderson would practice his partial repetitions from this range. In conversation with the authors, Anderson spoke highly of the effectiveness of the technique: "I've done them throughout the years. The first partial movement I did was the quarter squat. When I did them for a few weeks without doing full squats, I wanted to see what full squats would be like, so I started doing the full squats again and the weight felt like a feather!"

2. Ronald Walker, the great English Olympic weight lifter, developed his strength through limited range work to such a capacity that he could support more than 600 pounds overhead.

3. Anthony Clark, the first teenager in history to bench press 612 pounds, and the first man to reverse grip bench 701 pounds, told the authors of his experience with the partial reps principle: "I think they work! If you're doing heavy partials, that's providing a real

overload which causes a quick adaptation by the body...Once you go back down to a regular style of training with a lighter weight, it's much easier. I've used partials myself and, because of the length of the bar you can only really go slightly over 1,000 pounds, which I'll do on movements like squats and I'm around 800 pounds on the bench press."

4. Bill Kazmaier, whose numerous powerlifting championships and strong man titles earned him the additional title of being the "World's Greatest Strong Man," told the authors his thoughts about this great training technique: "I liked partials because of the overload they delivered...I did partial squats just to be able to handle the weight and also partial deadlifts to increase parts of the lockout. I did 1,000 pounds for partials in the squat as an assistance exercise and...they were very helpful in adding muscle mass." Strongest-range repetitions will do the same thing for the bodybuilder seeking increased muscle mass as it did for these champion lifters in search of greater overall body power.

Strongest-range repetitions build amazing ligament, tendon and muscle strength permiting the bodybuilder to perform phenomenally heavy bench presses, military presses, presses behind neck presses, along with a host of other power movements that build tremendous whole body power and very impressive muscular development.

Here are but three examples of how partial reps have stimulated, not only phenomenal power development, but also tremendous increases in muscle mass:

1. John Grimek, the legendary bodybuilder (and one of weight lifting's immortals as well), spoke to the authors about his experience in using partials to build not only colossal strength (remember, he was able to support overhead a 1,000 pound weight slung from

rafters on chains — at a body weight of only 185 pounds!) but also to develop his incredible muscle mass: "I had rafters in my attic to which I hooked up some support straps where a bar would be suspended from these rafters and loaded up with weights. You see, the straps would support the barbell at a height that was about eye level so that you could perform movements like partial presses overhead and so forth. I could really make my exercises very heavy this way. I recall that they worked quite well. In fact, I got quite strong using these, at least for my size and age and so forth. I was much stronger than anybody around at the time. It really increased my power and muscle mass quite a bit."

2. Mike Mentzer, the first bodybuilder to apply successfully the discipline of science to his training and also, not accidentally, the first ever to garner a "perfect" score of 300 in competition (1978 Mr. Universe contest, Acapulco, Mexico), was also a strong advocate of performing partial repetitions in his training. Mentzer had this to say to his audience in Muscle & Fitness magazine regarding his experience with partials: "The last time I engaged in any serious power rack work was when Casey Viator first moved to California in the late 1970's...in the quarter squat Casey and I both got up to more than 1,100 pounds for a few reps...we used 625 pounds for quarter reps in the incline press...we both used similarly impressive poundages in the deadlift and press behind neck. And while no one has ever accused either Casey or me of lacking size, we both noticed appreciable mass increases during that period of power rack work."

When Mike and his brother, Ray, were performing partial range preacher curls for their biceps back in the late 1970's he noted: "We would overload the bar for the preacher curls from our usual 150 pounds for full-range reps to 220 pounds for partial reps. Using a preacher bench perpendicular to the ground so the resistance didn't fall off in the top of the movement, one of us would lower the 220 pound bar to the halfway position where the other's hands would stop the bar, and possibly even give a slight boost to get the mammoth weight started back upward. Once the weight began its ascent no assistance was given. About four reps performed in this all-out fashion were all we could take. After a set performed in said manner we'd immediately sit down to avoid falling down!"

3. Lou Ferrigno, the star of The Incredible Hulk television series and one of the most massive bodybuilders of all time (6'5" and 320 pounds), is another champion who utilizes the technique of partial repetitions in his training, working up to 2,300 pounds on partial leg presses! Ferrigno had this to say about his experience with partials: "I used to do leg presses utilizing a full-range of motion, going all the way down to the point where my knees would touch my upper chest on every rep of every set. After a few sets of this, my lower back would be killing me but my thighs would have no pump at all. Eventually I started bending my knees just a bit and my thighs just went WHAM! My upper thighs blew right up! Eventually, they got up to 32 inches around!" It should be clear that strongest-range partial repetitions allow you to lift much heavier weights than you would normally lift and, of course, the heavier the weights you lift, the greater the overload you're imposing on the muscles, which is the prime requisite for building massive muscles. You've got to train heavy to get big, and partials allow you to train in the heaviest possible manner.

THE "WEAK LINK" ANALOGY

There is a popular maxim in strength training that states, "a chain is only as strong as its weakest link." In other words, you're only as strong in an exercise as you are in the weakest part of its range of motion. This is also known as the "sticking" point. This maxim, however, fails to take into account you have a choice in the matter; you don't have to train in your weakest range of motion. With full-range repetitions, you're restricted to how much overload you can impose on your muscles due to the leverage deficiency, even though your muscles are capable of handling, in most cases, hundreds of more pounds in the strongest range of the movement than you're presently subjecting them to.

If your muscles are capable of lifting 500 pounds for 20 repetitions and yet the most you ever work out with is 150 pounds for the same amount of reps, what reason does your body have to alter its present muscular size? Obviously none, even if you "progress" by adding one or two repetitions or even ten pounds to the exercise. The reason being that the level of muscular output is still well below what you're capable of. Yet, if you remain locked into the notion that you "must" perform full-range movements (usually because that's the way "everybody else" performs them), the maximum gains in the form of increases in strength and muscle mass that your body is capable of will never be achieved. Instead, you must think in terms of what your muscles are capable of handling in their strongest-range of motion, not their weakest one. If you remain training in your weakest range then you'll only progress as far and as quickly as your weakest link permits. If this is too slow, or if progress halts before you have reached your optimum muscularity, then you are a candidate for advanced strongest-range training.

STRENGTH, FLEXIBILITY AND ENDURANCE

The three benchmarks of physical fitness are strength, flexibility, and endurance. Precision Training is designed to accomplish one, and only one, of these objectives — strength. While certain weight lifting exercises could be performed in a manner (full-range) that may improve flexibility, and while an argument can be made that high repetitions with heavy partial movements can provide some stimulation to the endurance/cardiovascular system, such techniques would still be vastly inferior to yoga and running, or other specific stretching and endurance exercises. Using weight training to develop cardiovascular endurance could garner some improvement, but it could never equal cross-country skiing, distance running or other more specific exercises. Similarly, lifting weights through full or exaggerated ranges of motion could improve flexibility but never on the order of yoga or martial arts exercises. For developing strength, however, nothing can deliver better results than weight training, and nothing allows you to lift more weight safely than Precision Training in your strongest-range of motion.

POLEMICS FROM THE TRADITIONALISTS

Somewhere along the line you can expect to hear the disparaging statement, "With strongest-range partials you're not really as strong as you appear on paper because you're not doing a fullrange rep." This is an argument advanced only by people who enjoy arguing because, in reality, it's an argument that has no end. For example, the advent of cambered bench press bars that force your hands below chest level thereby allowing you to achieve an even greater range of motion than a straight Olympic barbell is capable of providing. But does this mean that all powerlifters are weak or "not really as strong as they appear on paper" because their range of motion is less with a straight Olympic bar than it is with a cambered bar? Further, there has never been a clinical study to prove that a full-range of motion is necessary in order to develop a "full" muscle. The fact is that humans nearly always work their muscles in a "functional range" that utilizes their maximum strength. That's why when you push a car your arms are almost fully extended instead of close to your chest. Or, as a trainee revealed to me on the phone the other day, why his two year old daughter can push him off the sofa with her legs. She naturally uses her strongest-range of motion. And you can be assured that her muscles will grow properly despite her not using a full-range of motion. Outside the gym, who does?

With strongest-range training, your muscles are made to contract against the heaviest weights possible and that is all that's required for maximum overload to be delivered to the muscles, and more importantly, the CNS. After all, the heavier the resistance the muscles are made to contract against, for as many repetitions as possible, the greater the growth stimulation that takes place.

10

THE TEN BEST EXERCISES FOR ADVANCED PRECISION TRAINING

The Advanced Precision Training Workout utilizes the same principles of exercise science and consequently uses almost identical exercises. These exercises all involve heavy compound movements that will tax a muscle or muscle group to its maximum ability. In short, these exercises require the highest Power Factor. Further, since they are performed in only the strongestrange of motion, they will generate the highest possible Power Factor under the optimum conditions for a given muscle or muscle group.

The Advanced Precision Training Workout is very strenuous. It is intended for the athlete who has been using Precision Training for several months and who has steadily progressed in his or her muscular size and strength but has finally reach a plateau that can not be surmounted. This seemingly final plateau is caused by the fact that when exercising through a full-range of motion a person will reach the point of lifting failure because of the limits of his or her weakest range of motion. For some athletes this final plateau will not matter as they do not require or desire additional muscular strength or size. But for those who want to acquire their maximum muscularity this plateau can be shattered by training exclusively in the strongest-range of motion.

When you first make the switch to strongest-range training you will note a large increase in your Power Factor and Power Index numbers. This is caused by the fact that you can lift heavier weight and, because you lift it a shorter distance, you can perform more reps per unit of time. Do not be overly impressed with the first big increase in your numbers as it is an "apples and oranges" comparison between full-range and strong range workouts. Remember, the Power Factor and Power Index numbers are used only as a relative indicator of your progressive overload and corresponding strength. Comparing numbers from entirely different workouts or from different individuals is meaningless.

Important Note: In order to perform strong range exercises safely it is MANDATORY to use either a power rack or a Smith machine in order to physically limit the range of motion. By definition, strong range training involves lifting weights that you are incapable of lifting in your weak range. Consequently, if the weight should be permitted to descend into your weak range, you will be powerless to move it and could suffer great injury. Use a power rack or Smith machine or do not perform these exercises.

WORKOUT "A"

When starting out perform four sets of 20 repetitions for each of the exercises that follow.

1. STANDING BARBELL PRESSES

The first exercise you'll be performing in Workout "A" will be standing barbell presses performed in either a power rack or, more preferably, a Smith Machine. The standing barbell press is a movement that will build extremely powerful muscles in your deltoids, traps and upper back. The Advanced Precision Training method of performing this exercise is as follows: First adjust the height of your support (whether in a Power rack or on a Smith machine) so that the bar is about two to four inches below the height of a fully extended rep. As soon as you develop a "feel" for the movement and are able to hoist some appreciable poundages, shorten up on your range with a two inch maximum in the distance the bar travels. From a standing position, with your hands approximately three inches wider than your shoulders on each side, press the bar upwards until your elbows are locked. Now lower the bar slightly, just enough to break the lock in your elbows, and simultaneously dip your legs in a simulated split position, i.e., one knee just slightly forward and unlocked while the back leg remains slightly bent. From this lower position, push/press the weight to the fully extended position, using some slight assistance from your calves and

Strongest range standing barbell press.

157

quads. This is really just a slight dipping movement, designed to assist you pressing that heavy weight upwards.

It is important to get a good quick cadence going with your reps in order to increase your work output in a unit of time, so don't be afraid to bang them out fast until you've reached 15 to 20 repetitions. If you still have plenty of gas left in your tank, head for 30 or 40. Rest as long as you feel you need to. Don't restrict yourself to 60 seconds or, worse still, 30 seconds, just because someone somewhere said that that is the right amount of time between sets. Your individual response to exercise, and the degree of systemic fatigue you experience from it, are highly individualized. Your recovery ability from an all-out set of strongest-range standing presses could well be closer to three minutes — or more! So train at your own pace as dictated by your Power Factor and Power Index numbers.

2. BARBELL SHRUGS

This exercise directly involves the trapezius muscles of your upper back as well as your entire shoulder structure, so the combined muscular effect will enable you to move some tremendous poundages. You will need to perform this movement in a power rack for total safety and confidence. It is strongly advisable to

Strongest range barbell shrugs.

get yourself a pair of heavy duty lifting hooks to be used during the performance of this exercise as the tonnage you'll be hoisting in this movement will mount up very quickly.

To begin this movement, first place the safety bars of the power rack in a position that allows the bar to rest two to four inches below your hands if you are standing up straight inside the power rack. Take an overhand grip on a barbell and, after establishing that your grip and your footing is secure, stand erect inside a power rack, thereby pulling the weight up off the pins. Your hands should be slightly wider apart than your shoulders. Once you're standing upright, begin to shrug your shoulders upward as quickly as possible with no pause at either the top or the bottom of the movement. Use a range of motion that is one half, or slightly less, than your full range. Again, get that nice quick cadence going — remember, the more work or reps you perform in a given set, the greater your muscle growth stimulation. Make the movement like a sprint with weights. Keep it going until you cannot draw the weight up even a fraction of an inch. Make sure to keep your arms straight at all times to ensure that your traps alone and not your biceps are doing the work.

3. CLOSE GRIP BENCH PRESSES

This exercise imparts tremendous overload on the triceps as well as pectorals and anterior deltoids, thereby stimulating phenomenal upper body muscle growth.

To start, place the safety bars of the power rack in a position that allows the bar to rest two to four inches below your full reach. When you are a newcomer to

Strongest range close grip bench presses.

strongest-range training, you can place the bar a full six inches under your fully extended reach. Once you're comfortable in handling the heavier poundages, decrease the distance of travel to two to three inches. Take a narrow overhand grip in the middle of a barbell (the outside of your palms should be just touching the inside of the knurling) and, lying on your back on a flat bench inside a power rack, raise the barbell off the pins and extend your arms upwards until they are completely locked out. From this fully extended position, bend your elbows slightly, just lowering the barbell an inch or two downwards, then push it back up to the starting position. Again, it's important to get a good cadence going with this exercise until you're at the upper limits that your individual Power Factor will allow.

4. PREACHER CURLS

Partial range Barbell Preacher curls will provide tremendous overload primarily to the biceps muscles of your upper arms and, secondarily, to your brachialis and forearm muscles.

To begin, take a shoulder width underhanded grip on either a cambered or regular barbell, anchor your elbows firmly onto the pad on the top of the preacher bench and keep them there throughout the duration of the exercise. The bench itself should be at a 90 degree angle (if possible) to the floor in order to insure maximum resistance in the fully contracted position. Lean back slightly to generate even more power. Either clean the barbell via "cheat curl" to your shoulders or, better yet, have a training

Strongest range preacher curls.

partner or a assistant, help you lift the barbell up into the fully contracted position for you. Lower the barbell slightly, about three inches, then immediately reverse the procedure and, pulling with biceps power alone, bring the barbell back up to the fully contracted position. As with all these exercises, pyramid your weight for each set until you have performed the last set to failure with the heaviest weight.

5. WEIGHTED CRUNCHES

Crunches are the best abdominal specific exercises. Your abs will get considerable use through their supporting role in the other exercises like standing barbell presses but if you really want to specifically target them, this is the exercise.

To begin, lie on your back on the floor with your

hands behind your head and your feet on top of a bench. Take hold of the "Crunch Strap" which should be attached to a low pulley. Try to keep your chin on your chest and slowly curl your trunk upwards towards a sitting position. Make sure you hold onto the strap tightly so that your abdominals are contracting maximally against the resistance. You'll find that you can only curl up a third of the range you would if performing a normal sit-up. This is fine because that is all the range of motion that your abdominals require to be stimulated into maximum growth. Once you have ascended to a fully contracted position, hold the position for a two count then lower yourself slowly back to the starting position. Repeat for the required number of repetitions.

That's the end of workout "A." You will notice with Precision Training a sense of deep tissue fatigue as opposed to a superficial pump. This fatigue is indicative of your muscles and the nervous system that supplies them, having been called upon to perform tasks that heretofore have never been attempted. You will also notice an increase in appetite and, when you go to bed,

Weighted crunches.

your sleep pattern will be deep and sound. When it comes time to repeat this workout, you will, if you took enough time off in between training sessions, be stronger. In fact, your strength, as measured by your Power Factor and Power Index numbers, should be increasing dramatically with every workout.

WORKOUT "B"

When starting out perform four sets of 20 repetitions for each of the following exercises.

6. THE DEADLIFT

This is the greatest exercise you can perform for developing the muscles of your lower back, buttocks, and hamstrings. Always keep a slight bend in your knees when performing this exercise in order to insure that your lumbar muscles, rather than your vertebrae, bear the brunt of the exercise stress.

Strongest range deadlift.

Start by placing a barbell inside the power rack at a height just slightly above your knees. Stand inside the power rack and grasp the barbell with a grip of approximately shoulder width. Your feet should be under the bar. Now slowly pull the resistance upwards, making sure to keep your arms straight, until you are fully erect and the barbell is resting on your upper thighs. From this fully erect position, lower the barbell smoothly, bending at the waist approximately four to five inches (if you're newcomer to strongest-range training) while keeping a slight bend in your knees throughout the movement. Then raise the weight back up to the starting position using only the power of your hamstrings, glutes, and lower back muscles. If you are already accustomed to the demands and mechanics of strongest-range training, shorten the range of travel to about three inches. You will find that, once the range has been shortened, you'll need even heavier weights to fully recruit the fibers of your spinal erectors, glutes, and even your deltoids. This is fine as training in your strongest range will allow you to exercise in the safest possible range of motion while the extra heavy weights employed will serve to recruit even more muscle fibers. The result is that the more fibers you can recruit, the more growth stimulation you'll be imparting. Once again, increase the resistance with each succeeding set.

7. THE BENCH PRESS

As most bodybuilders are aware, the bench press is a fundamental compound movement for the upper body and, when performed exclusively through its strongest-range of motion, will build incredible power, mass and strength into the pectorals, anterior deltoids, and triceps muscles.

Start by lying back on a flat bench inside a power rack. Set the pins in the rack to three to four inches below your full lockout reach. Place your feet flat on the floor for balance. Your grip should be medium width so

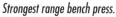

Strongest range bench press. *Strongest range lat pulldowns.*

that, as you lower the bar, your forearms are straight up and down (vertical). Raise the barbell from the pins and lock it out directly above your chest. With the bar directly above your chest, lower the bar until there's a slight bend in your elbows. Not such a bend that the barbell touches the pins in the power rack, but enough that it comes close to touching. Press the barbell upward until your arms are fully locked out again.

Repeat for four sets of 10 to 30 repetitions, adding weight with each successive set. Your rep cadence on this and all other exercises will be as quick as possible so as to attain your highest possible Power Factor and Power Index.

8. LAT PULLDOWNS

This exercise will widen your upper lats and put you well on your way to developing an incredible "V"-shape! It also allows you to utilize more weight than your body weight can provide which, for overload purposes, can prove to be a very desirable factor.

To begin, take a close underhand grip on the bar, sit on the seat with your knees hooked under the support. Your arms should be stretched fully above your head and the pull should be felt in both your lats and shoulder blades. Now pull the bar just slightly down, about three to four inches of travel then return it to the starting position. As you increase your weight, however, make it a point to reduce your range of travel, by just pulling on the bar and making it move two or three inches by the force of contracting your lats alone. Concentrate on making the upper back do the work and don't lean backwards to involve the lower back. Release the contraction and make a point of feeling the lats return to the fully stretched position.

9. LEG PRESSES

The leg press involves extensive use of the quadriceps, hamstrings and buttocks and is, because of the tonnage your legs can support in this movement, one of the best exercises that can be used in Precision Training. Leg presses permit the use of weight that is much heavier than most people can safely squat.

Strongest range leg presses.

To begin, sit down in a leg press machine with your back pressed comfortably against the angled pad and your buttocks on the seat bottom. Place your feet on the sled with your heels about shoulder width apart and your toes pointed either straight ahead or angled slightly outward. Straighten your legs and release the stop bars of the machine (or keep them locked if you are long legged). Grasp the handles beside the seat or the edge of the seat itself for better balance during the movement. Once the weight has been pressed upward and your straightened legs are just short of a full lockout, lower the weight about two to three inches then reverse the movement and press it back up to the starting position again. Never "throw" the weight upwards or let it "drop" downwards. Instead perform each and every repetition under complete control over the limited range of motion. If you're just beginning a range of four to six inches might feel more comfortable.

10. TOE PRESSES ON LEG PRESS MACHINE

This is a great exercise for the gastrocnemius and associated muscles of the lower leg as it allows you to pile on (in some instances) a ton of poundage!

To begin, sit in a leg press machine the same way you would if you were about to perform a standard set of leg presses. Place your feet on the platform and slowly push with your

Strongest range toe presses.

legs until your knees are locked out and your legs are straight. Once you have fully extended your legs, carefully slide your heels off the platform until only your toes and the balls of your feet remain in contact with it. Whenever possible, keep the machine's lock pins in place while performing this exercise as an added safety precaution in case your feet should slip off the platform. Keeping your legs straight, allow the weight of the machine to force your toes back slightly towards your body then contract your calves, completely extending your toes. The range here is limited to one or two inches of travel whether you are a beginner or an advanced trainee. Add weight each set duplicating the cadence and repetition scheme used in the strongest-range leg presses just discussed.

You're done.

Don't forget, train by the numbers and you'll make continual uninterrupted progress until you've reached the outermost limits of your genetic potential. And if that means only one workout every two weeks, so what? If that's what it takes for you to record a strength and size increase, then that's what it takes and there's no getting around it.

Remember, if you trained with sufficient progressive overload, you will be a stronger person when you return to the gym. Don't perform the identical workout next time as it will be too low an intensity for your increased strength.

12

YOUR IDEAL ROUTINE

Just what is the "ideal" training routine? How many sets? How many reps? How many exercises per body part? And, how many days per week should one train to stimulate maximum gains in size and strength? These are valid questions to be sure and, until recently, nobody had an answer to them. There were opinions — my goodness, there were opinions — but very few of these opinions were consistent and fewer still had any scientific basis in fact. When the authors looked into the realm of the requirements of productive exercise, they were surprised to find that the answers to these queries came forth readily, once time was taken to analyze the cause and effect relationship between size and strength.

When we embarked on the development of Precision Training, we did so with no preconceived biases or prejudices of how to train. No "opinions" were granted legitimacy. Instead, we went by what science had revealed to be physiological facts; things such as how our bodies react to stress, what exercises allow the use of the heaviest weights and, hence, yielded the greatest pounds per minute of exercise ratio (thereby allowing for the greatest amount of muscular output), what training methods delivered the greatest overload to the muscles, and how frequently such an overload could be applied to bring about a purely anabolic condition of the human body. These were our guidelines and, being factual, not subject to change but instead, straight-forward and black and white in their obviousness. We had no interest in the dogmatic preservation of body-building tradition or any other tradition for that matter. Our sole objective was purely rational; to discover exactly what was required in the way of progressive resistance exercise to produce the fastest possible results in both muscular size and strength.

Once viewed in this context, no other considerations held any meaning. It was at once obvious that in order to gain muscle mass, muscle growth had to be stimulated and, for maximum possible gains, there had to be maximum growth stimulation. At this point, the question became "How is muscle stimulated?' The answer came back "By imposing a progressive overload upon it." Another question then had to be asked; "Which tech-nique yields the greatest overload?" The answer to both queries, we discovered, was the technique of strongest-range repetitions wherein the greatest weight could be used to dramatically overload the muscles in a way that no other technique could even remotely approach. When the muscular overload in training is as high as possible, growth will have been stimulated and will indeed occur as long as your training sessions don't occur too frequently.

The whole idea behind lifting weights is to generate high- intensity muscular overload. If you were to just flex your elbow up and down, with no weight in your hand, your biceps muscle would not increase in size or strength. We lift weights in order to increase the intensity of work and trigger growth. But how is that intensity measured? It isn't. For over 100 years of strength training no system has ever quantified the amount of overload — until the Power Factor was innovated. Once a means of measuring overload is at hand, it becomes a simple task to quantify the value of every exercise and to guarantee that progress is taking place on a workout to workout basis.

The first thing the body does immediately after a workout is to recoup the energy and reserves that were lost during the workout. The processes of recovery and growth are separate, each requiring a certain amount of time. While recovery of an individual muscle may be quite rapid, the recovery of the overall physical system (also known as systemic recovery) was typically thought to require anywhere from 48 to 72 hours to take place. Recent research, however, backed up by the authors' personal experience would indicate that if the overload was of sufficient intensity to stimulate strength and size increases, a period of anywhere from one to six weeks may be required to elapse in order for it to manifest (during which time training again would be both unnecessary and counterproductive because it would have made further inroads into the individual's limited recovery ability). Again, if you are operating blind with no measure of your muscular output, you will have no accurate way to discern whether or not you have recovered from your previous workout. But, if ever you reach a point where you're not progressing in Precision Training, your Power Factor and/or Power Index will reveal it instantly.

Because you are stronger after each workout, your "ideal routine" changes every time. For example, we the authors, started our Precision Training on a three day per week split routine, wherein half the body (shoulders, traps, biceps, and triceps) was trained on one day and the other half (lats, pecs, lower back, legs and calves) trained on the next training day on an alternating basis. We would train on Mondays, Wednesdays and Fridays, allowing a full 48 hours to elapse (with an additional 24 hours on the weekends) between workouts to allow for the processes of recovery and growth to occur. For the first month and a half this spacing was perfect as our progress soared on a per workout basis. Soon an overhead press limit weight rose from a respectable 185 pounds to a monstrous 405 pounds. Likewise with bench presses; what had previously yielded six reps with 165 pounds was now, 70 days later, giving way to 485 pounds for 20 reps — and the leg presses just flat-out skyrocketed from 800 pounds for six reps to 1,325 pounds for 35 reps! Obviously some major changes had occurred for this to have happened. After all, weaker muscles (such as ours were when we started training) contracting maximally, do not require the same amount of metabolic fuel nor produce the same quantities of by-products and wastes as do stronger muscles contracting maximally and moving greater weights.

The result was that we were now so much stronger than when we began training, and our ability to generate maximum levels of overload had risen to such high levels, we were beginning to exceed our bodies' capacities to recover from our workouts. Our greater muscle mass (and we were gaining mass steadily), working at greater output levels, was using up much more fuel and producing much heavier quantities of waste products than we were even remotely capable of when we first started training. As a side note, total oxygen uptake in a trained muscle working at maximum capacity has been shown to increase in some cases up to 30 times its original resting capacity!

It was at this point that we began to experience a very strong disinclination to train on our scheduled three day per week program. We evidently had been stimulating growth with every workout, but due to the increased overload and corresponding increased demand on our recovery abilities, we apparently were not allowing sufficient time for both the recovery and growth processes to take place. All of this was reflected in a plateau then a decrease in our Power Index numbers. The only logical conclusion was that we would have to reduce our training days per week.

At this point, we reduced our Precision Training sessions to only two days per week (Tuesdays and Fridays) and sometimes even once a week. The result? Our strength gains made another quantum leap upwards! Our overhead presses were now being done with 475 pounds, our bench presses with 525 pounds for 20 reps, our repetition barbell shrugs with 600 pounds and our leg presses went over the moon to 1,600 pounds for 20 reps!

VARYING RECOVERY APPLICATIONS

As the effect of Power Factor Training is so dramatic upon the body, a prolonged recovery period is mandatory. The question at this point changes from, "How soon can I go back to the gym?" to "How soon must I go back to the gym?" Some individuals may only require one high-intensity Precision Training session per week in order to stimulate an adaptive response from the body depending on their innate adaptability to exercise.

Others may require two weeks off in between workouts for recovery and growth to manifest. And still others may require upwards of six weeks. What's becoming clear is that there exists a wide range of variation among individuals with regards to their personal recovery ability, i.e., their ability to tolerate peak overload training. By closely monitoring your Power Factor and Power Index numbers you can adjust the frequency of your workouts in such a manner that ensures either steady increases in size and strength or continual maintainance of your maximum strength. Any steady decline of Power Factor or Power Index numbers is an indicator of overtraining. One thing is certain if you are training with maximum overload, and if your workouts are both brief and infrequent enough (less than one hour) that you don't use up all of your recuperative reserves merely to compensate for the exhaustive effects of the workout itself, you will grow. The very fact that you grew stronger is proof that you fully recovered from your workout.

A WORD ABOUT REPETITIONS

Despite what some trainers will tell you, there exists no magic number of reps to perform for building mass or increasing definition. It should be remembered that muscular definition is primarily the result of losing subcutaneous fat so that the muscles directly beneath the skin appear in bold relief. To achieve this degree of definition, you really don't have to train with weights at all. Running even a mile a day will burn far more calories from your body than would the performance of some extra sets of bench presses or cable crossovers. In any event, it is well substantiated that training with peak overload causes the greatest adaptive response by the CNS. As long as you're training with your highest possible Power Factor and Power Index, you will have done all you reasonably can to stimulate an adaptive increase in your muscle mass stores. That should be the sole focus of your training — what gives me the higher numbers? The Power Factor and Power Index numbers are what is important, not whether you are doing eight reps, 12, 17, or 63.

While specific, one size fits all, repetition schemes are normally only applicable to a small cross section of the populace, it is of interest to note that research conducted back in 1956 by F.A. Hillebrandt and S.J. Houtz reported that when subjects engaged in lifting a weight that induced fatigue at 25 repetitions for up to ten sets, it produced a very profound effect in muscle tissue. They discovered that muscular output could increase by over 200% in as little as 15 training sessions. Such progress fits perfectly in line with what the authors have experienced when performing partial repetitions using heavy weights with similar repetitions in their Precision Training. According to Hellebrandt in his own conclusions, "...the living machine operates under such wide margins of safety that it is difficult to deplete hidden reserves of power in short periods of exercise consisting of small numbers of contractions." [16]

Although there is much merit in Hellebrandt's conclusions, you should still experiment with various numbers of sets and reps to see what combinations can give you your highest Power Factor and Power Index numbers using the above guidelines. As long as you don't train too often, no more than three times a week, you'll grow bigger and stronger from workout to workout.

LIFTING HEAVY WEIGHTS SAFELY

One of the stated objections to training with heavy weights is that "it's injurious to the bones and connective tissues." This objection is, however, without merit. Training with heavy weights is actually safe as long as the emphasis is on lifting the weight, as opposed to attempting to thrust it or torque it. Trying to move a weight that's simply too heavy for the muscles involved requires the use of "outside" forces such as momentum and body leverage. Lifting a heavy weight with the aid of these outside forces amplifies the force transmitted to the joints and connective tissues thereby increasing the risk of injury.

All exercises in Precision Training should be performed in strict form so that the involvement of these outside forces is eliminated. This is not to indicate that all your reps must be slow motion affairs, however. Studies have indicated that more fibers are involved utilizing a quicker rep cadence (at least on the concentric or lifting phase of the rep) providing that it is the muscle itself that is responsible for the velocity of the resistance and that the overload is under the total control of the muscle at all times. Once the velocity exceeds muscular control, the chances of injury are increased tremendously.

It is also advisable to obtain a good quality lifting belt that offers adequate support to your lumbar area for overhead lifts and other heavy exercises. In addition, we've found that wrist wraps and hooks are absolutely essential in movements such as deadlifts, pulldowns and shrugs as your muscular strength in the larger muscle groups will quickly surpass that of your smaller forearm muscles. When performing bench presses and overhead presses strong wrist wraps are mandatory.

13

BODYBUILDING – FACT VERSUS FICTION

Bodybuilding, as it is commonly practiced, is one of the least scientific endeavors in the sporting world. Not that bodybuilding can't be or is not scientific, but so few individuals have ever taken the time to learn about the actual sciences that comprise it, or how it ought to be practiced for maximal results.

Judging by some of the bizarre and downright fraudulent training beliefs that are currently in vogue these days, as well as by the volume of mail and phone calls we're receiving daily, it is safe to say that the time for a non-contradictory, rational and, most importantly, result-producing strength training system is long overdue. What follows is a solvent look at some of the more prevalent muscle building beliefs and what basis, if any, a person might have for holding them. You might be surprised.

ANGLE TRAINING IS A "MUST" FOR MAXIMUM MUSCLE DEVELOPMENT

"You've got to hit the muscle from different angles" is a popular belief these days. The so-called reasoning behind multiple angle training is predicated on the misconception that by training at different angles, you'll be bringing more muscle fibers into play that would not have been activated otherwise. Physiologically, this just isn't the case. More muscle fibers are not brought into play or recruited by changing such comparatively trivial mechanisms as hand spacing or the angle in which you recline your torso. In fact, if you performed an exercise that limited the stress of focus to only one region of a muscle group to the exclusion of all other regions then you would have reduced, by definition, the potential fiber involvement of the exercise and, hence, its productivity. The entire argument in support of multi-angle training as a means of maximizing muscle growth has missed the side of the barn by at least eight yards. The only factor that dictates muscle-fiber activation is how heavy the weight is — not the angle through which it's lifted. The heavier the weight, the more fibers are recruited to lift it, meaning that more fibers are stimulated to grow. Even if multi-angle training could effectively isolate certain sections of a given muscle, it would still be a step in the wrong direction since limiting the amount of fibers involved in a contraction would reduce the amount receiving growth stimulation. This is not what any bodybuilder's objective should be. For example, if incline presses could stress only the upper pecs (which they don't), then you would have only effectively stimulated one-third of your pectorals. This would require you to perform additional pec work to stimulate the remaining two thirds of your pecs. This is inherently inefficient. All in all, you would have to perform three exercises to stimulate one muscle complex — what a monumental waste of time! Particularly in light of the fact that both the upper and lower portions of the pec share a common tendon of insertion. The fibers in both regions are activated whenever the muscle complex is called into play.

It doesn't matter to the body whether you train with an incline bench, a decline bench or a flat bench. Your muscles can't differentiate between a barbell, a Nautilus machine or a bucket of rocks. All your muscles are concerned with is whether enough fibers have been recruited to move the resistance you're training with. Since it's your muscle fibers that do all of the lifting, it logically follows that exercises generating the highest Power Factor and Power Index numbers also involve the most muscle fibers. So, train by the numbers, not by preconceived notions regarding multiple inefficient exercises.

YOU'VE GOT TO "SHOCK" THE MUSCLE

The belief that you have to "shock" the muscle in order to make it grow is interesting, if only for its ambiguity. What could possibly be meant by this? Certainly if you actually "shocked" a muscle group you would have effectively left it incapacitated. Further, if you shocked your muscles and the motor units that supplied them, you're entire nervous system would be traumatized, not to mention your cardiac muscle! It should be remembered that muscle has one function and one function only: to contract. That's all that a muscle does. That's its sole function. Muscle isn't complicated at all. It's not like the kidneys. Muscle contracts or relaxes. That's it.

Given these two very restrictive parameters, what is the context of this "shock"? If, for example, you decide to "shock" your biceps muscle by having it perform a curl with a barbell instead of a dumbbell, its primary function, contraction, is still being carried out. So where's the shock? Likewise, instead of performing a dumbbell curl sitting up, if you perform it lying back on a 45 degree angled bench the action of the biceps muscle is still the same — it contracts. Again, that's its function. You cannot shock, coax, cajole, or the ever popular "confuse" a muscle into growth. In this last example, there's no such thing as a cellular brain in each individual muscle cell that would allow for it become "confused", "befuddled", "vexed," or filled with any form of angst. Muscle cells receive electrical stimulation from the brain via the central and peripheral nervous systems to either contract or disengage (relax) and that's it.

FULL RANGE FOR LENGTHENING THE MUSCLES

One of the more prevalent misconceptions in bodybuilding is the belief that a full-range of motion will somehow stimulate more muscle fibers near the insertion of a muscle. For example, it was commonly believed that if you performed full-range preacher curls for your biceps the stress of the exercise would be more directly focused onto the "lower biceps." This is ridiculous. Fibers, regardless of where they are located in a given muscle, are recruited and, hence, stimulated by one thing and one thing only — weight. Muscle fibers are recruited only as needed, which is to say, if the weight that you're attempting to lift has exceeded the capacity of those fibers already activated. Only then will more fibers be activated and they'll be activated irrespective of what part of the muscle group they happen to reside in. If you want to insure that all of the available muscle fibers in your biceps will be stimulated to grow bigger and stronger, then you have to employ a resistance that is heavy enough to recruit all available fibers. Excessive stretching or an exaggerated range of motion play no part at all in the muscle fiber recruitment process. It just isn't possible to lengthen muscles to any appreciable degree anyway. And certainly not by stretching them. Muscles are attached to bones by tendons, so the only way to lengthen a muscle would be to surgically cut the tendons and reattach them further down the bone. Muscle length is one of those genetic traits that just isn't subject to alteration. So, if your biceps aren't as long as Arnold's, forget about it and just focus on developing the best physique you can.

ISOLATION EXERCISES WILL CREATE DEFINITION AND STRIATIONS

If you ask most bodybuilders, professional or otherwise, why they perform several exercises for a given body part you'll usually hear a reply something like this: "Well, I perform my basic, heavy compound movement for size, another movement for shape, and a third to bring out the striations or 'quality'." Such an answer is absolutely loaded with fallacies. Apart from basic, heavy compound movements for size (they're also the ones that bring out a muscle group's inherent shape because they are the ones stimulating it into growth), there is no such thing as a "shaping" exercise or "definition" movement. It is the burning of calories beyond what you ingest in the form of calories that leads to the creation of definition. The more calories you expend, the greater the likelihood of your becoming defined. Therefore the exercises that burn the most calories, on a per set basis, are the ones that will lead to the creation of the greatest definition. And which exercises are these? The same ones you use to build maximum mass — heavy, basic, compound movements. Ask yourself in which exercise are the weights greatest and the muscular output required to move them the greatest — barbell bench presses with 200 pounds or repping out with a pair of 40 pound dumbbells for a set of flyes? Obviously the heavy benches would require far more energy to complete and would generate a higher Power Factor.

As far as striations go, skeletal muscle tissue is striated and everybody has skeletal muscle tissue. The term striated merely refers to the fact that the muscle is arranged longitudinally in bundles. When viewed under a microscope or with the naked eye on a highly defined bodybuilder, muscle striations are clearly visible. There would also appear to be a certain genetic predisposition towards striations; for example Mr. Olympia, Dorian Yates, has few striations whereas a tenth place finisher, Andreas Munzer, has them everywhere! Certainly Dorian Yates had every muscle group developed to its maximum on his body. In fact, his muscles were more fully developed than were Munzer's-and certainly both men were at incredibly low body fat levels, probably both in the neighborhood of 2%, yet, Munzer was the one with the striations. In conclusion then, you cannot train for shape or definition more successfully with isolation movements than you can with compound ones and striations are the result of both an incredibly low percent of body fat and a genetic predisposition towards such a condition. It cannot be "trained" into a muscle.

TWISTS WITH A POLE OR BARBELL WILL TRIM YOUR WAIST

Twists with either an empty barbell or a pole across your shoulders will do absolutely nothing to get rid of fat around your obliques. The reason is that the movement does not offer appreciable resistance even when performed at a quick cadence. The waist, or more specifically your obliques, receive no training effect from the exercise. Nor, for that matter, does the movement use up enough calories to burn any fat.

This all hastens back to the misconception of "spot reduction." That is, if you perform enough work on one specific area of your body, such as twists for your obliques, you'll "burn" away fat from that area. Actually, the fat loss process is a systemic one; you lose fat randomly from throughout the body — and even then only if you've burned significantly more calories through activity than you've taken in through food. When you go on a diet, fat is mobilized from all the body's multiple fat cells, not from isolated areas, such as the waist. Once fat has been broken down and mobilized it is transported by the blood to all the individual active cells in the body and burned for energy. The only way to get rid of fat from around your obliques is to go on a calorie reduced diet. If you stay on it long enough you'll eventually burn up all the fat in that area. In order to trim your waist and hasten the body's general fat burning process, it's recommended that you perform some form of aerobic activity, such as cycling, walking, jogging, or swimming. This combined with the Precision Training program to increase overall muscle tissue will trim your waist and assist in keeping the fat from returning.

THE FACTS ABOUT SUPPLEMENTS

One of the biggest concerns facing the bodybuilder of the 90's is the role of supplements. Never before has such an emphasis been placed on nutrition. Unfortunately, it is this very aspect of bodybuilding that is the most neglected. A contradiction? No, only an apparent one. It should be remembered that supplements and nutrition are two entirely different things. Nutrition is what we obtain on a daily basis from the foods we eat. Supplements, on the other hand, are only a factor when we're unable to obtain the "nutrition" our bodies require from those same foods. Supplements do play a role in nutrition when they're used as the term implies — supplementally. The single most important fact regarding nutrition for the bodybuilder, athlete, bowler, housewife, or anyone else who wishes to maintain health and build a strong body, is the unequivocal need for a well-balanced diet. A sound diet is one that provides daily all the nutrients (protein, carbs, fats, vitamins, minerals and water) necessary for maintaining health. Ironically, bodybuilders often forget that bodily health is the first requisite for building a muscular physique.

When you are unable to maintain a well-balanced diet, or if you suspect that you're deficient in a particular nutrient, then, and only then, can a case be made for resorting to protein powders, carb drinks and vitamin-mineral supplements. Remember, supplements were never intended to be used as foods or to replace them in the diet. When this has happened in the past, such as the liquid protein diets that were voguish back in the 70's, several deaths resulted. Again, supplements can only be justified when used supplementally; when particular deficiencies exist and can't be redressed by a closer attention to diet.

For example, bodybuilders who diet severely for a contest must be especially careful because reduced calorie diets are often so restrictive that the body does not receive many essential nutrients. Most nutritional scientists agree that a well-balanced diet becomes impossible once your daily caloric consumption drops below 1,500 calories per day. However, barring such conditions, the only thing supplements represent is a lack of attention to one's food selection and meal preparation. That, and a colossal waste of money.

THE VALUE OF B-15

Many athletes and bodybuilders receive vitamin B-15 shots. Some members of the bodybuilding community have been talking up this B vitamin as promoting muscle growth. And, while all vitamins do aid in the process of muscular growth, they don't do so directly. We all require a certain amount of all the various nutrients every day — not just vitamins — in order to maintain bodily health. There is no food substance which works directly in building muscle. You must first stimulate growth through your training in order to give the body's muscular system a physiological reason to alter its status quo. Only peak overload and a high rate of muscular output over a given unit of time will do this. Then you must provide your body with enough nutrition and rest to allow the growth you've stimulated to take place. So, to answer the question more directly, there is nothing magical about vitamin B-15 or any other substance, and certainly it doesn't take the place of hard work in the gym. Our advice in general to those seeking a "magic Potion" or "secret supplement" that will instantly hasten the muscle-growth process is to stop wasting so much time worrying about such things and invest your energies into peak overload workouts and proper nutrition.

THERE'S NO SUCH THING AS OVERTRAINING – ONLY UNDEREATING

One of the more recent misconceptions in body-building regards the issue of overtraining and nutrition. There is no such thing as overtraining, so it goes, only under eating. The implication here is that if you over-eat, you can accordingly extend the limit to which you can train and, hence, stimulate muscle growth. This position has absolutely no backing from exercise science. It should be remembered that the supply of biochemical resources used up in the process of growth stimulation are limited of necessity and cannot be restored instantaneously no matter how many calories you consume. Granted, nutrition does effect the degree to which growth can manifest, but to a limited extent. An adequate and optimal intake of nutrients serves to maintain a full supply of the biochemicals utilized in the growth process. Consuming quantities far in excess of that intake does not somehow force the body to expand this supply infinitely. The body has specific nutritional needs each day. The operative word being "needs." In the context of nutrition, the term implies a limit that cannot be transcended. It's like a bricklayer who needs exactly 4,000 bricks to build a chimney. He doesn't need 5,000. He doesn't need 4,050. And he doesn't need 4,001. He needs only 4,000 bricks. Likewise with nutrition; the body and its muscles have "needs" every bit as specific as the bricklayer — even more so, actually, as surplus bricks can be resold or, at worst, put aside until the next job. Surplus calories, on the other hand, those over and above what are required for maintenance and a little bit extra for the growth you may be stimulating from workout to workout, only result in the deposition of fat.

Therefore, the notion that forced feeding or hyper-nutrition can somehow compensate for the effects of what would otherwise be overtraining simply isn't true. Even at best, muscle growth is negligible on a daily basis anyway. A 30 pound gain of muscle a year — which would be wonderful — averages out to a little more than an ounce a day. An ounce! How many extra calories over and above maintenance levels do you think would be required for such a miniscule amount of growth to manifest? Damn few obviously. The evidence is that very little extra nutrition beyond what's required for maintenance levels is legitimately needed to gain muscular body weight on a consistent basis.

IN BODYBUILDING, THE AIM SHOULD BE TO "TEAR DOWN THE MUSCLE, THEN ALLOW IT TO BUILD BACK UP BIGGER AND STRONGER"

For decades, many bodybuilding authors and even a few exercise physiologists (who really should have known better) have been averring that weight training "tears down the muscles" and then you should take a few days off in order to allow the muscles to build back bigger and stronger. While on the surface it may sound plausible, in reality it just doesn't happen this way. Exercise cannot "tear down" or "damage" muscle tissue. If it did you wouldn't be able to leave the gym after an intense weight workout.

While there are some changes in muscle cell permeability as a result of an intense workout wherein there's a leakage of certain enzymes through the cell membrane, there are no dramatic alterations in the structural integrity of muscle fibers as a result of working out. Of course, this excludes the possibility of actual injury from accidental mishap during the workout. Proper bodybuilding training is geared to stimulate growth, not cause cellular trauma. In other words, the workout acts as a trigger mechanism that sets into motion a series of physiological steps that will, we hope, culminate in the production of muscle growth — providing certain preconditions, such as time for complete recovery and growth, are allowed to take place and adequate nutrition is consumed.

TRAIN FOR THE PUMP — THEN YOU KNOW YOU'VE STIMULATED GROWTH

Many bodybuilders head for the gym with the idea that "getting a good pump" is the key to muscle-growth stimulation. Unfortunately, there exists no evidence whatsoever that a pump is an index of muscle-growth stimulation. All bodybuilders achieve a pump to some degree every time they workout, yet, not all bodybuilders grow as a result of each workout. People who perform high-volume exercise, such as cyclists, joggers, and even Stairmaster enthusiasts, also experience a pump but don't experience growth as a result. If the pump was the sine qua non of muscle-growth stimulation then all of the aforementioned would be jumping up in weight classes on an almost weekly basis. A pump is simply edema; or the temporary swelling of tissue due to a fluid build up, in this case blood, in the muscle being worked. Unless growth was stimulated as a result of a workout, however, the muscle will revert to its previous size once the pump subsides. Strength training, which is what proper bodybuilding really is, doesn't always produce much in the way of a pump but there can be no mistaking the fact that, after a hard peak overload workout, the body is about to undergo some profound physiological changes. Increase your rate of work, or Power Factor, and your muscles WILL GET STRONGER. Therein lies the key to muscle growth as it was discovered a long, long time ago that muscular size and strength are directly related. More precisely, the strength of a muscle is proportional to its cross-sectional area. In other words, a stronger muscle is a bigger muscle. That's why when you remove a limb that's been immobilized due to injury from a cast, you notice that it's atrophied or become smaller from disuse. What's the doctor's prescription for rehabilitating that limb? To get those muscles to grow bigger again? Strength training! And the stronger the limb becomes, the bigger it becomes. Such is the nature of the relationship between size and strength and it can't be otherwise. Can you, for example, imagine a massively muscled bodybuilder like Paul DeMayo being able to bench press only 100 pounds? No, Paul works out with over 400 pounds on the bench press and he has the muscles to prove it. In other words, Paul is as big as he his because he is as strong as he is. If you want to grow bigger and bigger muscles, you should always train with an eye towards a strength improvement as reflected in your Power Factor and Power Index numbers. A pump, while a nice feeling admittedly, is not an accurate indicator of muscle-growth stimulation.

PLYOMETRICS

Another popular theory in training these days is that of plyometrics. This postulates that if you take a moderate weight but utilize explosive, fast repetitions, you'll stimulate only the "fast-twitch" fibers. This is yet another bit of fiction. Muscle fibers are recruited in an orderly fashion according to the resistance level they're being called upon to move. It's the heaviness of the weight to be lifted then, or more specifically, its force requirements and not the speed at which you perform the movement that recruits the fast-twitch fibers as the plyometric advocates would have you believe. To move a weight quickly it must be light because the lighter the weight, the quicker you can move it. Light weight, however, irrespective of the velocity through which you move it, only requires slow twitch fibers to accomplish the job. Demands of low muscular intensity are always met by the slow twitch fibers. Intermediate fibers come into play once the slow twitch fibers are no longer able to continue the task. The fast twitch fibers — the ones with the greatest mass potential — are finally recruited when the other two sets of fibers can no longer meet the force requirements. Therefore, when the fast twitch fibers are activated, all fibers are activated including the slow and intermediate twitch. And again, this recruitment process is not velocity dependent but force dependent; how much force is required to move the weight, with the heaviest weights requiring the greatest force and, hence, recruitment of fibers. Plyometric movements, with the light to moderate weights employed, cannot activate fast-twitch fibers. There simply is no evidence that movements performed in an explosive or ballistic fashion will — magically — bypass the slow and inter-mediate fibers in order to recruit solely fast-twitch fibers.

RETHINKING PERIODIZATION

Much has been written in the muscle magazines recently about the importance of "periodization" or "cycling" your workout routines throughout the course of a year. The authors of the properiodization articles liken bodybuilding to architecture. "You can't build a house without a blue print," they preach, "so you've got to map out your training plans accordingly." It's a cute metaphor admittedly, but somewhat incongruous.

After all, it would be an odd and infrequently em-ployed architect indeed who would propose dividing up the construction of a house into "seasons." Not to men-tion the fact that muscle cells are living organisms, not composed of pine and drywall and therefore cannot be treated as such. It was a cute metaphor, just not a very practical one.

As far as the concept of periodization itself is con-cerned, its advocates maintain that certain months of the year (or cycles) should be set aside for training with different weights, reps and, in some instances, goals, which its proponents tell you ahead of time are "required for ultimate success."

The truth, however, is that there exists no reason for periodization — particularly if you are a "clean athlete" (which we'll get to in a minute). It should be pointed out that the concept of periodization was created by the Russian Olympic lifting coaches in an attempt to synchronize the lifting of heavy weights with their lifters drug cycles (hence the term "cycling.") When they were on steroids and growth hormones, they were stronger and able to train much harder and heavier than when they were off the drugs. As a result, "periods" of heavy lifting were structured to coincide with their drug cycles then periods of lighter, less intense lifting were introduced into the schedule to reduce the chance of burnout and injury as the athletes came off the drugs. When the soviet lifters were winning titles, an American coach inquired about their "training system" and was told that they "divided the routines up into periods of heavy lifting along with periods of not-so-heavy lifting." In a perfect text book example of the "Post Hoc, Ergo Propter Hoc" fallacy, the US coach assumed that because their success came after following this "cycling" system, that had to be the result of following this cycling system. From this was born the entire "Periodization" concept, complete with its "Muscle Refinement Phase." If you really want for a days work sometime, try to look up this term in any muscle physiology textbook. You won't find it. It doesn't exist. You can do one of three things with muscle tissue: You can maintain its size, you can increase its size (hypertrophy) or you can decrease its size (atrophy). A bodybuilder seeking to increase his muscle size must first train hard enough to stimulate growth then rest long enough in between workouts to allow that growth to manifest. It's as simple as that. After all, this isn't crude oil we're dealing with, it's muscle tissue and, therefore, not subject to any process of "refinement." Muscle has one function; it contracts, and when it contracts against resistance that is increased on a progressive basis, it grows bigger and stronger.

Quite apart from the fact that the entire periodization concept is based on a misconception, is the fact that there's simply no evidence that engaging in activities that have been shown to have no effect on the process of muscle growth, such as training with lighter weights and reduced muscular output will, if it's "structured properly," somehow hasten the muscle-growth process. And what if you're feeling strong as a bull when you head for the gym and you know that you're capable of really setting some personal best records that day — but, it's the "Refinement Phase" you happen to be in this month and not the "Maximum Mass Phase" so you have to pull back on the throttle this workout. How does such gibberish result in anything accept spinning your wheels and reduced progress? The clinical formula for muscle growth is "increased work (overload) over a unit of time." Anything other than this will not stimulate muscle growth period.

FULL-RANGE SQUATS — THE BEST EXERCISE EVER!

Mark Berry, Hise and Perry Reader wrote volumes in the 1930s and 40s about the "wondrous, overall muscle building benefits of full squats." These beliefs have persisted to this day — and not without reason. According to men like Reader, who contributed much to the iron game, squats had a "stimulating effect on the entire system." He was right. Performing full-range squats — although a "weak range" exercise, did and will stimulate phenomenal overall muscle growth —

simply and only because the weights (overload) utilized in full-range squats is superior to the weights utilized in any other weak range movement. It wasn't the squats, per se, that stimulated this wondrous overall growth, but rather the fact that squats were the vehicle whereby heavy weights could be employed to tax the Central Nervous System sufficiently enough to cause an adaptive response. An even greater demand would have been placed on the CNS by the performance of strongest-range squats for the very same reason — heavier weights could have been employed.

Quarter squats would not only have produced greater muscle-growth stimulation but would have been much safer as well. Besides causing excessive shear forces in the knee joint, full-range squats cause severe compression of the spinal column, particularly in the bottom position, where the anterior aspect of the lumbar vertebrae is compressed. What happens is that the intervertebral discs end up getting pushed backwards which could result in either herniated or ruptured discs. Research has consistently revealed electromyographical activity of up to ten times body weight in the lumbar region when full squats are performed with as little as an individual's body weight. So while squatting may be a very productive exercise, if not THE most productive exercise, full squats are definitely not the way to go.

EXERCISE — HOW LITTLE YOU NEED!

Heavy overload exercise — the only kind that results in immediate muscular adaptation — is a form of stress to the muscles and the overall physical system. When performed properly such training will stimulate a compensatory build up in the form of additional muscle size and strength which aids the body in coping more successfully with similar stressors in the future. But bodybuilders who insist on training six to seven days a week (whether on a three days on, one day off or four days on, one day off system) will witness a decompensatory effect as the resulting drain on the regulatory subsystems of the body, and will actually prevent the build up of muscle tissue. All of the energy reserves will have to be called upon to attempt to overcome the energy debt caused by such overtraining.

These facts strongly indicate that the less time spent in the gym, the better your results will be. You'll find that your results will be spectacular if you limit your total training time to one, two or — at the most — three workouts per week of roughly 45 to 60 minutes per session. Although recovery time will vary from individual to individual, most people starting out require a bare minimum of 48 hours in between workouts in order to recover and grow stronger. As the trainee grows stronger, however, the less training his body will be able to handle before actually becoming overtrained and catabolic. When you use Precision Training you will have the ability to see the extent to which you have recovered through analyzing your Power Factor and Power Index numbers. If you return to the gym too soon after a workout you will not perform as well and your numbers will reflect this. When this happens, just add a day or two of recovery until your numbers show some improvement.

Like all other physical characteristics of humans, the time needed in between workouts in order for complete recovery and growth to manifest will vary widely between individuals. After identical workouts, one person may be able to return to the gym in 48 hours and see an increase in his Power Factor and Power Index numbers, while another person may need as many as eight weeks to go by in order to recover sufficiently and show improvement. Hard to believe, you say?

Consider the following: The May 93 issue of the Journal of Physiology reported that a group of men and women aged 22 to 32 took part in an exercise experiment in which they trained their forearms in a negative-only fashion to a point of muscular failure. Negatives are considered by some exercise physiologists to be more important than positive (concentric) contractions owing to the fact that more weight is able to be employed. In any event, all of the subjects agreed that they were most sore two days after exercising and that the soreness was gone by the ninth day. But it took most of the people nearly six weeks to regain just half of the strength they had before the workout! The study concluded that muscles are drained far more severely by intense exercise than was previously thought.

According to this research, it can literally take months for the muscles of some individuals to heal and adapt after an intensive workout. It is clear that the spacing of workouts, then, can be measured along a range of time that begins with the first day you can return to the gym and expect to see an improvement and ends with the last day you can return to the gym and expect to see an improvement. Precision Training will allow you to precisely determine your personal range of recovery ability which, depending on a variety of personal factors, may be anywhere from a few days to many weeks.

Regardless of what your personal range of recovery happens to be, one thing is for certain — everyone's personal recovery ability takes much longer to complete itself than was initially thought and training more than three days a week — and maybe even once a week — is going to be a mistake for most bodybuilders who are looking to increase their muscle mass.

PRE-EXHAUSTION

No matter how much a muscle is used, it will not grow larger or stronger until it is overloaded. This means that the intensity of the work required of it must be increased above what it is currently accustomed to performing. That is, it must be required to exert more power or work against a greater resistance than before. According to exercise physiologists, who make their careers out of studying closely the cause and effect relationships of such things, hypertrophy, or the increase in the crosssectional area of a muscles fibers, can best be triggered by increasing both the amount of weight lifted (overload) and the rate of work or pounds lifted per minute -the Power Factor. The higher the overload and rate of work, the greater the adaptive response of muscle growth. It is the Central Nervous System that triggers the growth process, a process that cannot be called into play by the isolated and protracted performance of highly repetitive tasks that are of a level well within the body's existing muscular capacity.

The fact is that growth is systemic in nature and the trigger mechanism that signals the body to grow can only be turned on by a "Call to Arms" from the Central Nervous System. Growth isn't easy, it must literally be forced to occur. Such being the case, how does one force growth with light weights or mild exertion? The answer is one can't — at least not without growth drugs. Taking the preceding facts into consideration, it becomes much easier to evaluate all training methodologies, including one that gained a tremendous amount of exposure and popularity during the 1970's — the pre-exhaustion principle. Pre-exhaustion became so popular that Arthur Jones, the much-heralded creator of Nautilus Exercise equipment, designed several of his machines with an isolation/compound component built into them in order to take full advantage of it. For the sake of illustration, pre-exhaustion requires that an isolation movement be performed prior to a compound movement with, literally, "zero" rest time in between the two. The fact that isolation movements necessitate that lighter weights be used than would be utilized in compound movements is enough of an indicator to tell you that this system is heading in the wrong direction. Second, if it's a full-range isolation movement, the weights are reduced even further. Therefore your muscles are performing less work (moving less weight) over a given unit of time — per set.

That's just for openers. When the compound movement is performed immediately after the isolation movement, the resistance must also be reduced in order for the temporarily fatigued muscles to continue to contract. Usually this resistance is in the neighborhood of 50% less of what the trainee would normally use. Again, a reduced resistance. Given that the clinical formula for hypertrophy is increased work in a unit of time, pre-exhaust is a step towards doing less work (less total weight lifted) in a unit of time. Sure you're doing two sets back to back — but with lighter weight. Additionally, the reps performed in pre-exhaust total out to roughly six to eight per set which is a total of 12 to 16 — or roughly half the amount of reps performed in one strong-range set — with much less resistance. The result? Little or no muscle growth. Granted, muscle can be stimulated to grow using methods such as pre-exhaustion, but only minimally. Maximal stimulation cannot be obtained with such a system owing to such a reduced level of muscular output that such training engenders.

Here's a further illustration: A typical pre-exhaust cycle would see a bodybuilder perform dumbbell flyes and bench presses for his pecs. If the bodybuilder could normally bench press 200 pounds for ten reps, then he should be able to start his dumbbell flyes fresh with a pair of 50s. That's 100 pounds total times ten reps which equals 1,000 pounds of muscular output. Next he performs barbell bench presses with 50% less weight than he is capable of, or 100 pounds. Given that his pecs are fatigued at this point, he might be able to eke out another ten reps (if he's lucky) for an additional 1,000 pounds of muscular output. Probably he wouldn't get ten reps, but we'll give him the benefit of the doubt so that his work over a unit of time (the clinical formula for hypertrophy) is up to 2,000 pounds.

On the other hand, if this same bodybuilder can full-range bench press 200 pounds for ten reps, then experience reveals that he can easily strongest-range bench press that same weight for 60 reps, making for a total weight lifted of 12,000 pounds or exactly six times the muscular output or work over the exact same unit of time. Now which of these two methods would have the greatest impact on the CNS? Which of these two methods would send out the greatest call to arms for more muscular growth 2,000 pounds or 12,000 pounds of muscular output?

And the truth of the matter is that this individual's rate of lifting through strong-range training would be much higher as he could lift far more weight than 200 pounds for even more reps which would result in a further increase in his rate of work over a unit of time or muscle growth. According to the Law of Muscle Fiber Recruitment, the heavier the weight, the more muscle fibers are called into play to move it. Conversely, the lighter the weight, the fewer fibers that are required to move it. Knowing that the pre-exhaustion system incorporates lighter weights and reduced muscular overload, is not nearly as efficient a muscle building system as some advocates might have initially believed.

STEROIDS

First, to state that steroids only add perhaps 10% of polish to one's physique, as some bodybuilders do, is perhaps the biggest joke in professional bodybuilding. It is, unfortunately, more like 90% of everything you see. This is unsettling for a number of reasons, not the least of which is the fact that these drugs are illegal. Beyond that, however, is the fact that if they can get their results out of a pill or bottle, then they have no vested interest in trying to determine just what kind of progress can be made without the drugs.

It's a medical fact that if you take large quantities of anabolic steroids — and don't train, your muscles will not grow. If you train with a large quantity of muscular output, however, and don't take any anabolic steroids, your muscles will grow. Granted, if you also take anabolic steroids and train properly, your muscles will grow even larger but still, the foregoing reveals the interesting fact that training — not drugs — is the key to turning on the muscle-growth process. This was verified by studies conducted at Harvard University over 20 years ago in which Doctor Alfred Goldberg and his colleagues discovered that if adequate stimulation is present, muscle tissue will grow. Further, they noted that it will grow quickly and in proportion to the severity of the stimulation and in the absence of influences such as testosterone, growth hormone, insulin, and even food! Stimulation then, is the first requisite. Steroids play a secondary role in the muscle-growth process. Yes, they do work but doesn't it give pause for thought that, if the right kind of stimulation is present, muscle will grow and continue to grow if that stimulation remains present. As no bodybuilder has yet trained over an entire career with a precise means of monitoring his results to insure that such a level of stimulation was present, it still remains to be seen what he ultimate limits truly are for the drug-free human body.

AMINO ACIDS

It's absolutely amazing just how many bodybuilders readily accept the notion that amino acid supplements are somehow a primary requisite in the muscle-growth process.

The history of amino acid supplements can be traced to a few years back, when protein supplements became, for a time, rather unpopular with the body-building community due to scientific information being disseminated by biochemists, physiologists, and nutritionally informed bodybuilders, such as Mike Mentzer, who insisted that a well-balanced diet provided more than enough protein for the aspiring bodybuilder and that supplements were, by and large, simply a waste of money and the body's energy in digesting them.

At this point, the protein manufacturers, in an

attempt to recapture the tremendously lucrative protein market, reissued the protein supplements — only this time with a new name "Amino Acids." It's simply another example of old wine in new skins, as amino acids are simply the nitrogen based constituents of protein and, consequently, yield the same effect as their soya, milk, egg, and beef predecessors.

Of course, not only did the labels change but also the marketing strategies employed to promote the "new" products; amino acid supplements were now accompanied by ad campaigns declaring that they were actually safe, effective, and even superior replacements to anabolic steroids — which is tantamount to telling a man who is testosterone deficient that all he needs is a good protein shake in order to set things right. It is at once obvious that such claims were ludicrous; after all, protein is a nutritional element whereas a steroid is a hormone. There exists no similarity between the two at all. While one is a dietary consideration the other is a drug. There is a big difference between the two.

It should also be noted that while amino acids are absolutely necessary for proper bodily and muscular function, including muscle growth, whether they're in the form of a capsule, a pill or a T-Bone steak makes no difference at all to your body, which simply breaks down the macro-molecule of protein into its constituent amino acids and redistributes the individual amino acids to where they're needed most. Unlike the sugars that enter the blood from carbohydrates, however, each amino acid retains its distinctive chemical structure in order to be utilized to make up the varied sequences and structures of human proteins.

It must be remembered that the body has specific needs for protein and additional amounts, such as those obtained through supplements, serve no biological value. As long as the cells have all the amino acids they need, regardless of how they were consumed, additional amino acids will not be put to work. Making more amino acids available will not make cells multiply or renew at a faster rate. Pouring excess amino acids into your body is no different than giving a contractor more lumber than he needs to build a house.

The genes that shape our bodies — and particularly our muscular development — provide each cell with instructions for making proteins from amino acids. These instructions must be precise. For a small change in amino acid sequence or structure can make a protein unusable — or even lethal. The method by which the trillions of cells in the human body encode and use this information has been known since 1962 when Watson, Crick, and Wilkins discovered how the instructions for making the more than 100,000 proteins of the body were carried in every cell by a tiny amount of DNA — a discovery for which they were awarded the Nobel Prize that same year.

These cells determine what proteins have to be made then signal the chromosomes in the nucleus that a specific protein is needed. DNA itself is a chain of nucleotides, each of which is made of sugar, a phosphate and a base. It's the sequencing of the nucleotides in DNA that actually instructs the cells in how to make the various proteins that the body needs. The DNA nucleotides are partly made from a sugar called deoxyribose from which DNA takes its name. The free-floating nucleotides are made with the sugar ribose; the chains which they eventually make up are known as ribonucleic acids or RNA.

Because RNA relentlessly seeks out only amino acids,

and because we know that all molecules of any one amino acid are completely interchangeable, we can conclude that for protein synthesis the food source of the amino acids does not matter. For example, if the amino acid lysine is what the DNA blueprint calls for, the transfer RNA will seek lysine and nothing else without concern for whether that lysine molecule comes from a hot dog, a can of tuna, sunflower seeds, soy sprout or an amino acid supplement. Further, lysine from one source cannot be different from that of any other; if it were, it could not be used.

There is evidence that we really do much better when the amino acids come from foods as opposed to supplements. Apparently, the complicated mechanisms of absorbing amino acids from the intestine require that some amino acid chains be present. When attempting to maintain the nutrition of the ill, especially those who have digestive problems (such as post surgical patients), it has been found that pure amino acids taken by mouth are not that well absorbed. When liquid foods (which are used for patients) are formulated with a mix of some pure amino acids and short chains there seems to be better absorption.

Again, amino acids are not a requisite for building big muscles. To build big muscles you must first stimulate muscle growth at the cellular level via peak overload training then allow sufficient time to elapse between workouts in order to allow your muscular reserves time to recover and grow. Then and only then does nutrition become a factor in the growth process. Adequate nutrition of all nutrients and not just protein or amino acids must be provided in order for you to maintain your existing level of muscle mass and, if you stimulated growth by training with sufficient overload, a little bit extra (approximately 16 calories with a protein breakdown of .9 grams per kilogram of body weight) must be consumed in order to allow that growth to manifest.

A well-balanced diet that is comprised of two or more portions of what was formerly known as the Four Basic Food Groups; cereals and grains, fruits and vegetables, meats and dairy products, and consumed daily will provide you with sufficient nutrition to both maintain your health and, if you've stimulated it, allow for the growth of additional muscle mass. However, there is no way that amino acid supplements can by themselves either stimulate or accelerate the muscle-growth process.

INSTINCTIVE TRAINING

There is a very loud school in bodybuilding which advocates that you must "trust your instincts," as opposed to science, when it comes to building muscles. "Go with your gut," they say. The funny thing is that they actually mean it! Never in his wildest dreams (and some of them were pretty wild indeed) would Sigmund Freud, the father of modern psychiatry, have ever postulated that our species has a "bodybuilding instinct." An "instinct" to build big muscles in order to ultimately rub baby oil on them and go up on a stage and pose? I mean, it's downright laughable. Even if such an instinct did exist, and the premise of man being an instinctive creature is by no means granted here, attempting to monitor ones results by such a subjective index as how you felt at any given time would, in the final analysis, yield you nothing. I could feel that I was having the greatest workout of my life — but if my Power Factor and Index numbers were down, I'd be grossly mistaken. Only in bodybuilding could one postulate such a ludicrous hypothesis as "instinctive training" and get away with it. Could you imagine, for example, an Olympic sprinter trying to monitor his progress by "feel" or "instinct?" Of his never having measured his progress by using a stopwatch? Or of never having any tangible, objective measure of the effects of his training techniques nor of his improvement from one month to the next? And yet this is exactly the kind of irrational, low-tech methodology that bodybuilders have always used.

Until Power Factor Training came on the scene, no objective gauges by which to accurately measure one's progress, or lack thereof, had ever been applied to bodybuilding. Power Factor Training allowed bodybuilders to measure and find the optimum point where they could sustain their highest workload or Power Factor and, hence, their greatest degree of muscle-growth stimulation — the effectiveness of which showed up in their workout numbers. Feeling something to be true, is no guarantee that it is true. NASA doesn't employ individuals who simply have " a good feeling about aerodynamics" to plot out their space programs; they hire people with bona fide scientific backgrounds who understand and can objectively measure the means of successful space travel. And so it is in any endeavor that science is involved including bodybuilding. Or, at least it should be. After all, it was science, not instinct, that sent men to the moon, cured disease, controlled the environment, and determined how muscle growth is really stimulated.

THE SEVEN MYTHS OF BODYBUILDING

■ MYTH # 1: BIG MUSCLES WILL SLOW YOU DOWN

Many coaches and personal trainers believe that an increase in the size and strength of a muscle will result in slower movements when performing a particular athletic event. Boxing, for example, always maintained that weight training would slow down the punching speed of the boxer. But just the opposite takes place. The speed at which you can perform a particular movement will be enhanced tremendously by increasing your strength levels. The speed of a body movement is dependent on two factors: 1) The strength of the muscles that are actually involved when performing a specific skill and 2) your capacity to recruit muscle fibers while performing the movement (neurological efficiency).

It's fallacious to assume that a muscle will "slow down" by increasing its strength and size. The correlation between the speed of a muscle movement and the strength level of the muscle are positively related. Therefore, to increase the speed of a muscle movement, increase the strength levels of the muscles needed to perform that particular movement.

■ MYTH # 2: ALL THAT MUSCLE TURNS TO FAT EVENTUALLY

This is perhaps the most common misconception in bodybuilding (particularly to the non-bodybuilder) and is distinguishable only by its being totally divorced from reality. Muscle can no more be turned into fat than an apple can be turned into an orange; they are two entirely different cells — one cannot "magically" become the other.

If you were to chemically analyze fat and muscle, you would discover that muscle and fat both contain varying amounts of protein, water and lipids, and inorganic materials. When muscle is exercised, however, it contracts and produces movement, whereas fat will not contract and is usually stored in the body as a source of fuel. It is physiologically and chemically impossible to convert a muscle to fat and vice-versa.

A simple explanation of what takes place can be illustrated by observing the ex-athlete's pattern of exercise and caloric intake. When an athlete stops training his or her muscles, the muscles will begin to atrophy or "shrink" from disuse. At the same time, the athlete will continue to consume the same level of calories. With the athlete consuming more calories than are needed to maintain his or her body weight and energy demands, the excess is then stored in the body as additional fat. If an athlete becomes obese after terminating a strength training program, it is due to caloric imbalance; i.e., taking more than they're burning off, and not muscle transforming to fat. Some individuals believe that their body weight should maintain a constant level upon the termination of a strength training program. Unfortunately, these individuals fail to understand that if they lose ten pounds of muscle mass through muscle atrophy and their body weight remains the same, then the weight loss that is attributed to muscle atrophy has been replaced by deposits of additional fat.

Thus, upon stopping one's training, one should also alter his or her calorie intake.

■ MYTH # 3: LIFTING HEAVY WEIGHTS IS BAD FOR THE JOINTS

For one thing the term "heavy" is a relative...heavy compared to what? Nothing can be evaluated without standards for comparison. And, in Precision Training, the only person who's standards are of significance for comparative purposes is you.

Properly performed, Precision Training, using what for you are considered "heavy" weights will actually strengthen the muscles that surround each joint which serves to actually make the joint more stable and less susceptible to injury. Proper overload on the ligaments and tendons in the joint region actually serves to thicken them (much the same as a callous forming on the hands), making them far stronger than they ordinarily would be. Such a practice must, however, be dealt with cautiously. A greater potential for injury lies, not in performing heavy strongest-range training movements (which are within the body's most advantageous leverage and muscular range), but in full-range movements that subject the joints and connective tissues in their weakest position, thereby exceeding (often considerably) the structural integrity of said joints and connective tissues. Extreme stretching of joints can, in fact, cause very real damage to ligaments and tendons.

■ MYTH # 4: YOU HAVE TO TRAIN WITH HEAVY WEIGHTS AND LOW REPS FOR MASS, AND WITH LIGHT WEIGHTS AND HIGH REPS FOR DEFINITION

Some articles in bodybuilding magazines have stated that, "Eight reps builds mass, twelve reps builds definition." This myth just won't go away. Muscle mass is built by forcing your muscles to exceed their normal maximum output, measured in pounds per minute lifted, irrespective of the number of reps it takes. Muscular definition is primarily the result of dieting off subcutaneous fat so that the muscles directly beneath the skin appear in bold relief. To achieve such a degree of definition, you really don't even have to train with weights. Running a mile a day will burn far more calories from your body, and remove far more fat, than would the performance of an extra set of bench presses or cable crossovers.

■ MYTH # 5: YOU HAVE TO WORK A MUSCLE THROUGH A FULL-RANGE OF MOTION IN ORDER TO FULLY DEVELOP IT.

It should be noted that nowhere has there ever been a study that stated that a full-range of motion is a requisite to stimulating maximum muscle growth. The contention of some that partial or strongest-range movements aren't as effective as full-range movements because you're only lifting the weight a few inches is a view that is totally unsupported by science.

Muscle-fiber recruitment (and, therefore, growth stimulation) is a matter of force requirements and not flexibility. The range of motion, therefore, is not a factor in the muscle-growth process. If it were otherwise, then yoga masters and contortionists would be the most muscularly massive individuals on the planet. In other words, if you can lift heavier weights, you will recruit more muscle fibers regardless of the range you use to lift it. The body isn't concerned about such aesthetic factors as whether or not your biceps have extended "all the way down" on a preacher curl. In terms of its energy systems, the body can't tell if you're training your quads or your pecs; its sole concern is how much energy and fiber recruitment are required to move that tremendously heavy weight at the end of your arms.

When your muscles have suddenly been called upon to lift a very heavy weight for a lot of repetitions, a tremendous amount of energy must be created — quickly. The body, then, concerns itself with factors such as muscle fiber activation, hormone secretion, increased blood flow to the working muscles, clearing waste byproducts as quickly as possible, initiating the Krebs cycle and a host of other metabolic activities. With strongest-range training, the two requirements for inducing hypertrophy (maximal overload and increased work in a unit of time) are brought to bear on the skeletal muscles in a manner that no other training method can even remotely approximate.

■ MYTH # 6: REAL GAINS IN MASS AND STRENGTH WILL COME WHEN YOU LEARN HOW TO "FEEL" THE EXERCISES YOU PERFORM AND TRAIN "INSTINCTIVELY"

The issue as to whether or not man is an instinctive creature is one best left to the realm of philosophy and psychology. To postulate that man, however, somewhere in the innermost recesses of his psyche, possesses some sort of a "bodybuilding instinct" or "training instinct" is downright ludicrous.

Even if such a thing did exist, attempting to monitor one's results by such a subjective index as how you felt at any given time would be tantamount to having no way of monitoring one's results. Can you envision an athlete in any other sport engaging in his training in such a nebulous, haphazard and subjective fashion?

Could you imagine, for example, an Olympic miler trying to monitor his progress by "feel" or "instinct" while experimenting with running techniques like wind sprints, intervals, running hills, etc., and never measuring his progress by using a stopwatch? Of never having any tangible, objective measure of the effects of his training techniques nor of his improvement from one month to the next? And yet this is exactly the type of low-tech methodology that bodybuilders have always used. There has always existed a technological barrier to finding out the validity of training beliefs and methodologies.

No objective gauges by which to accurately measure one's progress, or lack thereof, have ever been applied to the sport. In their place are maxims such as "no pain, no gain," "high reps for definition, low reps for mass," "incline presses for your upper pecs," and "muscle confusion," with no objective method to measure their efficacy.

What makes Precision Training revolutionary is its ability to measure and find the optimum point where you can sustain your highest Power Factor (and, hence, greatest degree of muscle-growth stimulation) while accumulating your highest total weight. This is achieved by determining the best combination of weights, reps, and sets for each exercise you perform. Results can then be calculated, and even graphed, to immediately reveal the effectiveness of your workout. This new found technology negates the need for "cookie cutter" routines that prescribe predetermined numbers of sets, reps and weights irrespective of the tremendous physical and physiological variation between athletes.

■ MYTH # 7: YOU SHOULD NEVER TRAIN LESS THAN THREE-DAYS PER WEEK OR ELSE YOUR MUSCLES WILL GET SMALLER.

The issue of training frequency still is cause for debate among individuals (including supposed authorities) in the realm of bodybuilding. Even solid writers such as Arthur Jones and Ellington Darden, PhD., who have injected liberal doses of much needed sanity into the realm of bodybuilding, still have some unwarranted suppositions (and not a little dogma) in their conclusions. One of these areas is in the realm of training frequency.

Darden writes that a three day per week routine is best regardless of your level of development. His reasoning being as follows: "A first workout is performed on Monday, a second on Wednesday, and a third on Friday. On Sunday your body is expecting and is prepared for a fourth workout, but it doesn't come." (pg. 161-162, 100 High-Intensity Ways to Improve Your Bodybuilding). What exactly is this? Certainly not science. The biceps muscles don't talk to the triceps muscles midway through Sunday afternoon and say, "Wasn't there supposed to be a workout today? I was kind of expecting a workout today. I mean, it's been 48 hours and we had one every 48 hours ago."

To our knowledge, there is nothing in the scientific literature to suggest that muscle tissue thinks (despite the misapplied term of "muscle memory" to the condition of reconditioning an atrophied muscle) by any manner or means. Muscle tissue, you'll be pleased to note, is wonderfully uncomplicated. Muscle tissue will do one of three things: Atrophy (from disuse), hypertrophy (from overload training and rest), or remain the same (from genetics and mild stimulation). Technically, muscle action is even more simple; they either contract or relax depending on the neural impulse they receive. It's that simple.

Rather than waste time trying to outwit non-thinking tissue into growing bigger and stronger, the simple solution to building muscle, once you've stimulated growth through heavy overload training, is to take adequate time off in between workouts to recover and allow the growth you may have stimulated to manifest (again: stimulate, recover, grow). Your Power Factor and Power Index numbers will instantly reveal to you whether or not you need more time off in between workouts by virtue of their increasing (in which case, you're doing fine and your frequency of training is perfect) or decreasing (in which case you haven't allowed enough time for recovery and growth to take place).

Trying to pigeon hole your physiology into responding to a three day per week program — once it's obvious that you're no longer gaining on such a system, simply because Arthur Jones at one time believed this to be the best way to space out workouts is tantamount to no reasoning whatsoever.

To further illustrate the nature of the recovery process, it might help to take a look at some of the actual research that is being done in this field.

The May 93 issue of the Journal of Physiology reported that a group of men and women (ages 22 to 32) took part in a physiology experiment in which they trained their forearms muscles to a point of muscular failure. All of the subjects agreed that they were most sore two days after exercising and that the soreness was gone by the ninth day. But it took most of the people nearly six weeks to regain just half the strength they had before the rigorous exercise. The study concluded that muscles are damaged more severely by intense exercise than was previously thought.

According to this new research (which corresponds perfectly with what we've discovered with Precision Training), it can take months for muscles to heal from an intensive workout. Remembering the tri-phasic nature of the growth-process (stimulate, recover, grow) such evidence strongly suggests that the time needed to recover from a workout that actually stimulates growth can be well over the six week mark. Then, once the recovery process has taken place, an additional block of time must be taken to allow for the growth that was stimulated, some six to seven weeks back, to manifest.

This may sound incredible, particularly to people who've been trained in the traditional bodybuilding methods that have them training three to six days in a row without a break. But it must be remembered that muscle growth can only be stimulated by all out, severe (for want of a better term) training and such training simply takes time to recover from. And the greater the severity of the training (the heavier the weights you're using and the greater the muscular output), the greater the period of recovery must be. And, as we've just learned, it can take upwards of six weeks.

Much of the confusion regarding training frequency might arise from the fact that bodybuilders confuse the low-intensity, low muscular output feeling of aerobics (highly repetitive, daily activity), which causes some pumping or edema of tissue but is perceived by the body and the Central Nervous System as a very low intensity activity. And rightly so. While it's true that you can stand literally hours and hours of daily low-intensity activity, the same cannot be said of high-intensity maximum overload activity which is the kind necessary to stimulate maximum gains in muscle mass. It is a case of apples and oranges.

Precision Training is not aerobics or yoga and, consequently, the recovery periods following a Precision Training workout must be protracted simply to allow the growth you've stimulated to take place.

Incidentally, in some of his more recent writings, Arthur Jones has advanced the notion that training three times per week is probably less effective than training once a week would be. He's drawn this conclusion based on his own empirical observations and some carefully considered conclusions. But then, it was never Jones who was all that dogmatic about his conclusions. It was his followers. Jones, to my recollection, always stated that his research was a paradigm until contrary evidence proved it outdated or incorrect.

Nevertheless any claim to truth without evidence or data cited to back it up is simply predicated on the logical fallacy of "Appeal to Authority." When unwarranted claims supersede all else — even empirical evidence to the contrary — such information ceases to become science (which is always amenable to reason or evidence). Science, if it is to be truly an intellectual movement, cannot be planned by any central authority; it has to be open to refinement and extension. Once it becomes a closed system, impervious to research or modification, it ceases to be "Science" and instead becomes dogma.

In conclusion, you don't need to "shock" or "confuse" your muscle cells to get them to grow bigger and stronger. You only have to subject them to progressive overload and give them adequate rest afterward.

14

QUESTIONS AND ANSWERS

SUBSTITUTING EXERCISES

Q: Sometimes I like to perform other exercises. Can I substitute other exercises for the ones that you recommend?

A: Any exercise that involves lifting weight can be adapted to Precision Training. The same principles of a Power Factor and Power Index apply to any weightlifting exercise. We have chosen the recommended exercises because of their efficiency and their ability to achieve maximum overload. For example, if your triceps muscles are capable of a 3,000 pound per minute Power Factor on close grip bench presses what would be the point of performing cable pushdowns for your triceps when it only generates a 1,500 pound per minute Power Factor? Be sure to ask yourself that question before spending a lot of time on little exercises.

TOO STRONG FOR MY LEG PRESS

Q: I do Advanced Precision Training and I am now capable of leg pressing over 2,000 pounds. The problem is that the gym I use has a leg press that only goes up to 1,600 pounds. Any ideas?

A: Believe it or not, this is a common problem when training in the strongest range. The authors ran into this problem during the development of Power Factor Training and we have received phone calls and letter from people all over the world with the same dilemma. The best tactic when you reach this stage is to train one leg at a time. This effectively doubles the capacity of the leg press machine. The first time you switch to one leg at a time it will completely change your Power Factor and Index numbers but that is OK because you just keep applying the progressive overload principle. Also, be careful to properly center your foot on the leg press machine so that the movement does not cause injury.

TIME KEEPING

Q: I work out with a partner and we do the same exercises one after the other. Should we each keep track of our time separately?

A: The most important factor in time keeping is consistency; do it the same way every time. As a practical matter the time it takes your partner to perform say, a set on the bench presses is about the same amount of time you would be resting between sets anyway so just using one stopwatch is fine. It you want exactitude, however, use one stopwatch for each partner. The point is that you need to do it the same way every time so that you get an "apples to apples" comparison of your performance from workout to workout.

GETTING READY FOR A CONTEST

Q: I am a bodybuilder getting ready for a contest. Can I still use Precision Training before a contest?

A: Another common question that points to the confusion surrounding bodybuilding. What is your objective when getting ready for a contest? If you want to add or maintain muscle mass then lift weights. If you want to get "cut up" then do aerobics. Your muscles don't care if your getting ready for a contest or not. They grow when progressively more overload is present and they do not grow when it is absent. Nothing changes that, not the time of year, not diet, not a "mass phase" or "refinement phase" (see next question.) Your muscles grow when you create stimulation for them to grow. You get "cut up" or muscle "definition" by losing bodyfat.

Q: Much has been written in the muscle and powerlifting magazines recently about the importance of cycling your workout routines to prevent overtraining. They say that you have to do this in order to stress the muscles differently and "shock the muscles" back into growing again. They also advise that doing so gives the body a break from heavy workouts which, according to them, lead rapidly to overtraining and that low intensity workouts will "refine" the muscles. What is Precision Training's response to this?

A: The Precision Training response is the same as that of enlightened exercise physiologists. We reject the theory of cycling or "periodization," wherein you reduce overload intensity in favor of increasing the length and frequency of workouts, as is postulated a requisite for building muscular mass and strength. There is simply no evidence that engaging in activities that have been shown to have no effect on the process of hypertrophy will, if they're scheduled a certain way, somehow enhance the hypertrophy process. People who advocate the "need" for periodization are ignoring the fact that muscular overload must be progressive in order to trigger adaptation. For example, if you are capable of lifting 5,000 pounds per minute in your bench press routine, what would be the point of several weeks or months of lifting 3,000 pounds per minute? How could that possibly trigger growth or "refinement"?

A properly conducted Precision Training routine also compensates for the stress on the body because it's carried on only for brief periods and includes adequate time for recuperation and growth between workouts. Proper application of the Precision Training System requires a maximum of no more than three workouts performed on three non-consecutive days each week (such as Monday, Wednesday, and Friday) which further allows adequate time for full recovery and growth to occur. In fact, one of the authors, Peter Sisco, was forced to take a six week layoff after injuring his back performing a full-range clean and press with 225 pounds. During that period, he also had the flu and was inactive. When he returned to the gym six weeks later it was with the full intention of doing a very light workout "...just to get used to training again." As soon as he started to train, however, he realized that the protracted "off time" had filled his muscles with a recharged power — more power than he had ever displayed previously! His strong range overhead press weight went up to a phenomenal 510 pounds while his bench press weight shot up to 600 pounds — a full 75 pounds past his previous best! A similar increase, though not nearly as dramatic, occurred for John Little; he too was forced into a four week period of relative inactivity. When he returned to the gym, his strong range overhead press went up to 415 pounds for a triple whereas before he couldn't even get 400 pounds off the pins! His bench press went up to 540 pounds for a triple!

What these results reveal, along with the observations of Mentzer and Sherman and the clinical studies of exercise physiologists, is not only that trainees need a lot less time in the gym than has been universally believed (particularly by the "periodization" or "cycling" advocates), but that peak overload on a progressive basis performed over a given unit of time is the sole factor responsible for muscle growth. Strategically predetermining certain months in which to reduce your muscular overload, and to perform higher reps alternated with periods of moderate intensity with moderate reps, or any other such reduction in muscular output, is an absolute waste of time as far as stimulating increases in size and strength are concerned. Knowing these facts regarding the requirements for muscle growth, there exists absolutely no excuse for the serious bodybuilder or powerlifter to train with less than all out effort each and every workout.

Incidentally, periodization got its start when Eastern Bloc Olympic coaches began the use of steroids for their athletes. The human body cannot withstand the massive doses of the drugs on a continual basis so training intensity was reduced during the periods of no drug use and increased during periods of heavy drug use. This "cycling" of lifting intensity was erroneously taken as the reason for the great strength increases. In truth it was the drugs that had to be cycled, not the training intensity.

CAN'T COMPARE INDIVIDUALS

Q: Can I compare my Power Factor and Power Index to someone else's?

A: The simple answer to your question is "no." There are many reasons for this, a few of which deserve some elaboration. Many bodybuilders and strength athletes refuse to believe that size and strength are related. To support this erroneous contention, they will invariably point to two individuals and note that one of them is smaller and less massive than the other and yet the smaller individual can lift more weight. A contradiction? Only an apparent one.

What they've failed to consider in their example is the fact that accurate comparisons between individuals such as this cannot be made as there exist just too many independent variables to consider before drawing such a broad conclusion. It may very well be true that the smaller individual has a 16" arm and can curl 150 pounds, while the larger one has an 17" arm and can curl "only" 135 pounds. The point here is that the individual with the 16" arm will be stronger than he was when his arm has grown to 17 inches because that size increase will be due to increased muscle strength. Likewise the bigger individual will be stronger than he was when his arm measures 19 inches. In some instances, the variance in strength can be due to leverage differences, i.e., the smaller arm has shorter bones in it and thus lifts the weight a shorter distance, thereby providing the smaller individual with a decided advantage in demonstrating strength.

Another contributing factor could also be the existence of favorable attachment points. For example, if one individual's biceps tendon is attached closer to the elbow joint he will have a pronounced leverage advantage. Other factors influencing strength development are things such as neuromuscular efficiency. A cubic inch of one individual's muscle may be capable of producing more power than a comparable amount from another individual's.

Because of these and other differences between individuals, meaningful comparisons are difficult to make. Comparisons are best made only by the individual measuring himself over a given period of time. The Power Factor and Power Index are intended to be used only as a relative indicator of whether or not your muscular overload and corresponding strength are increasing.

PRECISION TRAINING — THE LOGICAL CHOICE

Q: Why is Advanced Precision Training more effective than other forms of training?

A: Advanced Precision Training is the most effective training method simply because it delivers the highest overload to the muscles. Further, this system also takes into account the physiologic principles of recovery and growth after this superior form of overload has been applied. When these two aspects of training have been followed the net gain is always superior and progressive results.

Knowing this, it further stands to reason that the most productive training method for a person to utilize in his quest for optimum strength and muscle size is that of Precision Training. This doesn't mean that all other training methods are bad, nor that unless you use Precision Training you're doomed to failure. Conventional training methods deliver some results, to be sure, because they do provide some form of overload to the muscles. What they don't provide, however, is maximum overload to the muscles and a precise, mathematical method of gauging both muscular output and progress. Only Precision Training provides these.

BODYBUILDING APPLICATIONS

Q: I'm a bodybuilder and, while I like to lift heavy weights, I'm wondering what difference developing strong ligament strength in addition to muscle strength will have on my physique.

A: To get the most out of your Precision Training, you should never neglect the exercises that build up the strength of the connective tissue and that accustom the body to the handling of extremely heavy poundages. The only way to obtain this power is through handling the heaviest possible poundages over short ranges of muscle action and, obviously, through the utilization of exercises that work the largest muscle groups of the body such as the thighs, the back, shoulders, chest and arms.

In addition to increasing overall strength and mass, toning up the muscles and connective tissue, a Power Factor Training program also increases confidence and enthusiasm. By handling extremely heavy poundages, a positive mental outlook and sense of achievement are created, and the poundages you used in ordinary movements that seemed so heavy, will appear as light as a feather after your Advanced Precision Training routine. (should you decide to return to conventional training that is!).

THE DESIGNER GENES OF A CHAMPION

Q: If I engage in Precision Training, will I become a champion bodybuilder?

A: There are many factors to consider when answering your question, not the least of which is genetics. As an example, no one would dispute the fact that being tall certainly would influence your chances of being a successful professional basketball player (all "Spud" Webb types notwithstanding) nor that the exact opposite would be true for someone who wanted to be a professional jockey. It's obvious, however, that bouncing a basketball or running up and down a court won't have any effect upon your height, nor will riding a horse all day long make you a shorter individual. Your height in both of these cases is determined by your genetics. Genetics also play a role in the success or failure of champion bodybuilders, namely their genetic potential to develop inordinately large muscles. Two of the more important factors in determining a muscle's size potential is the length of a given muscle — from the tendon attachments on each end and the fiber density of the muscle itself. The longer the muscle, the greater the cross-sectional area when contracted, and thus the greater volume that muscle has the potential to reach. If you have extremely long muscle bellies throughout your entire physique, then, rest assured, Precision Training will help you realize all of your genetic potential and, if you also have the mental discipline, you could well become a champion.

YOU'RE NEVER TOO OLD TO TRAIN

Q: I'm very interested in increasing my power and muscle mass. However, I'm over 50 years of age and honestly believe that I am too old to benefit from your system. Is there another activity that you can recommend for "old timers" like me?

A: While we can empathize with your concerns about returning to training after a lengthy lay off, we cannot at all agree with your conclusion. A University of Southern California study involving a group of 70 year-old men showed significant improvement in muscular strength after an eight week strength training program. This serves to underscore the fact that you're never too old to start strength training. It should be remembered that bigger muscles are stronger muscles and stronger muscles contribute to any movement activity. Additionally, improving posture and elevating your metabolism allows you to burn body fat more efficiently, helping to prevent injuries. Stronger muscles also mean more stable joints which, as we get older, are usually the first areas to lose support and suffer pain.

With regard to your question regarding another activity, we're inclined to recommend Precision Training. Not only are your joints, muscles, and connective tissue strengthened by proper Precision Training, but it produces benefits much more efficiently than does, say, walking or swimming, in a third of the time. Regardless of your age, if you can move a limb, even a couple of inches, then you can move it against resistance and stimulate your muscles to grow stronger. But be sure your physician gives you the okay first before resuming any vigorous exercise program.

STRENGTH VS. SPEED

Q: Even though I believe what you said about "a stronger athlete being a better athlete," I'm not sure that a stronger athlete makes a faster athlete. I need speed in my sport (martial arts). Will Precision Training be able to deliver it?

A: Absolutely! A stronger athlete is a "faster athlete" precisely because of the increased strength factor. Look at it this way; let's say you want to press a 100 pound barbell overhead as fast as possible. If your deltoids, traps and triceps muscles are capable of combining to press 102 pounds, then your speed of movement with 100 pounds will obviously be very slow. It might even take five to six seconds to move the weight to the locked out position. On the other hand, if the involved muscles are capable of pressing 200 pounds, you'll be able to press the 100 pound barbell in half a second and, in all probability, maybe even less time. If your pressing ability is 250 pounds, then your speed of movement will be even more rapid. As skill is not significantly involved in pressing a barbell, the increase in speed is obviously due to the strengthening of the muscles. If all else is equal, the stronger individual will also move the fastest as he will have the greatest muscle mass to body weight ratio. After all, if you add more horsepower to the engine of an automobile, it will move faster.

DOWNPLAYING PROTEIN

Q: How important is protein in building muscle?

A: When most of us think we're not gaining fast enough, our first inclination is to increase our training time (which to a point is good but, beyond which, leads to overtraining) and to increase our protein intake. It should be stressed right off the top that neither of these things will hasten the muscle-growth process. In fact, they actually retard the development of muscle tissue. Most of us think that muscle equals protein. When you think of protein, you think of muscle tissue and, when you think of muscle tissue, you think of protein. There's no scientific reasoning for this belief, however, as muscle tissue is comprised of 70% water, only 22% protein, 6% lipids and other fatty acids and 2% inorganic material. Looked at in this light we can see that the primary constituent of muscle tissue is not protein, but water!

Does this mean that we can hasten the muscle-growth process by drinking gallons of water every day? No, but this is the often the irrational conclusion drawn by bodybuilders and other strength athletes who are looking to increase their size and strength. They operate under the assumption that if muscle is protein, then the more protein we eat the faster we grow. Now that we know muscle is comprised mainly of water, it might appear obvious to these people that we should drink great amounts of water in order to hasten the muscle-growth process. But you may have learned from first-hand experience that when you drink more water than your body requires the excess is passed out of the body through the urine. A similar condition exists with protein; if you fill yourself up with a lot of unneeded protein, the body utilizes as much as it requires and the rest is metabolized and excreted. Unlike water, though, protein contains calories and any excess calories not required by the body are stored as fat. Extra calories from protein are just as fattening as calories from carbohydrates or fat. It's the excess of calories, like those found in protein supplements, that make you fat.

THE NEED FOR CARBOHYDRATES

Q: How important are carbohydrates in bodybuilding?

A: Apart from water, carbohydrates are the most

important thing you can take into your body, not only for building larger muscles, but for your body to remain healthy. The primary nutritional consideration is always to make sure you're getting a balanced diet, but you cannot overlook the extreme importance of carbohydrates. Any kind of anaerobic activity, which is what Precision Training is, demands sugar as fuel. It's an erroneous notion that you can lift weights to get "cut up" or defined because weight training does not burn fat as fuel (at least not if training for increased size and strength is your goal). Weight training burns sugar and if you're not getting sugar from fruits and vegetables, or cereals and grains, how are your muscles going to continue contracting? The only way they can continue to do so is through a process of converting stored protein from the body into sugar. There's an amino acid contained in your muscle tissue, called Alanine, which will be broken down in your liver and converted to glucose. In other words, your body will start feeding on your hard-earned muscle tissue to obtain the sugars necessary to fuel muscular contraction. That's why carbohydrates are referred to as "protein-sparing;" they spare your protein stores (or muscle tissue) from being broken down and used as a source for energy.

LEANER MEANS STRONGER

Q: Don't you think you're stronger when you're heavier, even though that extra body weight isn't all muscle?

A: No, absolutely not. Rather than helping body strength, any excess fat actually hinders body strength. Some studies performed on overweight individuals have revealed that intramuscular fat (fat found in between muscle fibers) actually hinders the process of muscular contraction as it serves to create intercellular friction. This has the effect of making you weaker than you otherwise would be if your cells were unobstructed. In other words, the leaner you are, the stronger you are.

REALISTIC EXPECTATIONS

Q: How much muscle mass can you expect to build in one year of Precision Training?

A: It has been said that, if you are lucky enough to gain ten pounds of muscle in one year, then you can consider yourself most fortunate. But in light of the results we've been seeing in Precision Training that belief may now be obsolete. For example, in one week of Advanced Precision Training, John Little gained 10 pounds after having remained at a body weight of 180 pounds for over ten years. One might be tempted to say that he probably ate more during that week and trained less, therefore he gained 10 pounds of fat. This was not the case, however. He didn't alter his diet in any way and his waist size remained the same while his Power Factor and Power Index all went up dramatically indicating a pronounced increase in strength. As noted elsewhere in this manual, a stronger muscle is a bigger muscle and, of course, a bigger muscle is a denser, heavier muscle. The only reason for the increase then was obviously the adaptive bodily response (muscular overcompensation) to the superior overload imposed upon it from his Precision Training. It should be noted that Little put on an additional ten pounds over the next four weeks (12 workouts) as his Power Factor and Power Index increased on a per workout basis. Perhaps for the majority of trainees who still cling to other less intense methods of training, ten pounds per year is a more realistic expectation, at least during the first few years.

If you think that ten pounds per year isn't much (especially in light of the high set, seven day per week training methods most bodybuilders employ), just imagine how little it actually is when measured on a day to day basis. With 365 days in a year, the daily amount of muscle growth amounts to only .027 pounds, which is less than half an ounce. That's not even enough to register on a body weight scale! With Precision Training the trainees make palpable, measurable progress on a consistent basis and, as evidenced by Little's success, it's not uncommon to gain upwards of 15 pounds in under a month.

"TRAINING FOR DEFINITION" — A MISNOMER

Q: I want to put on muscle size as quickly as possible without putting on any fat in the process. In fact, I'd like to lose a bit of body fat too. How do I train for size and definition at the same time?

A: First, you can't train for definition. Most people, when referring to definition training, mean long, arduous hours of low-intensity work which does not build size but, instead, endurance or cardiovascular efficiency. In order to build size you must do just the opposite which means that training must be intense, infrequent, and relatively brief.

One of the basic concepts of exercise physiology is specificity which means that your body will adapt to achieve only one of these goals but not both. We all possess what the late stress physiologist, Dr. Hans Selye, referred to as adaptation energy, and this adaptation energy must be spent 100% for either building size and strength or endurance. As a result, it would appear that your double-edged objective could be more efficiently obtained if, rather than divide this energy between the two, you trained specifically for size and simply reduced your caloric intake in the pursuit of definition.

MORE ON VARIABLE ANGLE EXERCISE

Q: How can you say that by performing only bench presses I'm hitting all aspects of the chest, i.e., upper, middle and lower?

A: I checked my muscle physiology textbooks before making the statement. To use your very example, I'll admit that the upper pec has nerves stimulating it that are not involved in the contraction of the lower pec and, as a result, many bodybuilders have come to the errone-ous view that the chest, being composed of at least two distinct muscles, requires different exercises to ensure that all aspects of the pec are trained. But these two portions of the pec share a common tendon of insertion and the fibers in both portions are called into play to-gether whenever the primary function of the pec is called into play, i.e., the drawing of the arms towards the mid line of the body as they are in a close-grip bench press. Benching on an incline or using a wide grip, may "feel" like it's affecting the outer or upper portion of your chest and close-grip benches may "feel" like they're really focusing the stress of the movement upon the inner pec, but what you really feel in both in-stances is a far cry from what is actually taking place. What you are feeling is nothing more than the physical stretching of your pec muscle and surrounding tissue which causes the pain sensors in that vicinity to respond. This is a physical sensation that has nothing to do with stimulating growth in these distinct regions and really shouldn't be thought of as an indicator of that particular exercise's region of affect.

The function of the pectoral muscles is to move the upper arms down and across the midline of the torso. The exercise that comes closest to fulfilling both of these functions is the decline barbell bench press. Similar results can be obtained, however, with flat bench work and, as more of these benches exist in homes and gymnasiums, we've opted to utilize this exercise as our primary chest movement in Precision Training. In all honesty, the ability to completely isolate portions of a given muscle group is almost impossible anyway, since synergistic and stabilizer muscles are almost always called into action during any exercise that involves a given muscle group.

A FINAL WORD ON INTENSITY

Q: In most of the books and articles advocating a "high-intensity" approach to training, the authors will go on at great lengths about the necessity of training with high intensity. What exactly is "intensity" as it refers to bodybuilding?

A: Intensity, as evidenced by the writings of Mike Mentzer, Arthur Jones, Ellington Darden, and many other high-intensity advocates is a word familiar to virtually anyone who has studied, not only their writings, but any form of weight training or spent time in a gym. Most current trainers speak of the need for their clients to train with "high-intensity," however, it is a term that is both variously and loosely defined.

It has been used to refer to any workout that consists

of low repetitions and the heaviest possible weights. It has also been used to connote any body part exercise that is done to deep muscular fatigue. The Nautilus and Heavy Duty advocates believe that any workout in which you use 100% of your momentary effort is the proper denotation of the term, while still others will tell you that any workout that simply leaves you feeling thoroughly depleted is a high-intensity workout. While all of these definitions have varying specific applications, they all hint at the same key to building muscle-overload. Overload is the indispensable condition in the process of building muscle. Precision Training, using partials, provides a unique form of overload! It provides the highest possible overload in your muscle's strongest possible range of motion. And, measuring over the same range of motion every time, the Power Factor and Power Index will indicate, clearly and unambiguously, the relative output of your muscles and the increase in your strength.

ENDNOTES

1. Cooper, Kenneth H., M.D., M.P.H. with Sydney Lou Bonnick, M.D., "Aerobic Exercise, Strength Training, and Bone Mass," published in the book entitled "The New Fitness Formula Of The 90's," published by The National Exercise For Life Institute, © 1990

2. Morpurgo's research (Ueber Activitats-hypertrophie der wikurlichen Muskeln., Virchows Arch. 150, 522-544, 1897) was corroborated by the experiments of physiologists such as W. Siebert and H. Petow (Studien uber Arbeitshypertrophie des Muskels, Z. Klin Medl, 102, 427-433, 1925 and Untersuchungen uber Hypoertrophie des Skellet-muskels, Z. Klinl Medl, 109, 350-359, 1928), Leeberger (Professor of Physical Education, University of California, presented his findings at an annual meeting of the A.A.H.P.E.R. in 1932, Barnett, Holly and Ashmore Stretch-induced growth in chicken wing muscles: biochemical and morphological characterization. American Journal of Physiology, 1980. 239:C39-C46, Atherton, James, Mahon

Studies on muscle fiber splitting in skeletal muscle. Experientia 1981, 37:308-310 and Gollnick, Timson, Moore and Reidy

Muscular enlargement and number of fibers in skeletal muscles of rats. Journal of Applied Physiology 1981, 50:936-943) to name but a few.

3. Lange, Ueber Funktionelle Anpassung USW, Berlin, Julius Springer, 1917.

4. W. Seibert and H. Petow (Studien uber Arbeitshypertrophie des Muskels, Z. Klin Medl, 102, 427-433, 1925).

5. Dr. A. Steinhaus, (The Journal of the Association for PHysical and Mental Rehabilitation, Vol. 9. No. 5, Sept-oct., 1955, pg. 147-150.)

6. Studies by D.H. Clarke (1973) published in Exercise and Sport Sciences Reviews, 1:73-102 and by P.V. Komi, J.T. Viitasalo, R. Rauramaa and B. Vihko (1978) in the European Journal of Applied Physiology, 40:45-55, have demonstrated that unilateral training produces a bi-lateral strength increase which, they feel, is directly related to the influence of the Central Nervous System (C.N.S.) upon the musculature.

7. Mike Mentzer in conversation with John Little (tape recording), November 1992.

8. Stephen Kiesling, describing Michael Sherman's research on Marathon Runners in the January 1985 issue of American Health magazine.

9. Mike Mentzer in conversation with John Little (tape recording), November 1992.

10. Research conducted by H. S. Milner-Brown and colleagues empirically validated the fact that the load imposed upon muscle during contraction is the major factor dictating the type and volume of muscle fiber recruitment. The results of their research were written up in Journal of Physiology, Vol. 230, pg. 359, 1973.

11. S.Grillner and M.Udo Acta Physiol Scand, Vol. 81, p.571, 1971.

12. H.S. Milner-Brown and Colleagues, Journal of Physiology, Vol. 230, p. 385, 1973.

13. D.H. Clarke in his article Adaptations in strength and muscular endurance resulting from exercise, Exercise and Sport Sciences Reviews 1973, 1:73-102.

14. This is common knowledge to any student of anatomy and physiology. My referent was from Human Physiology, chapter six, pgs: 79-90, 1972, Morrison, Cornett, Tether, Gratz.

15. Dr. Fred Hatfield, Bodybuilding: A Scientific Approach, Contemporary Books, c 1988, pg. 34.

16. F.A. Hellebrandt and S.J. Houtz (Phys Therapy Rev, vol. 36, p. 371).

Blank

ACCESSORIES

Here are some accessories that will help you get more out of your training. These products have been selected by Power Factor Publishing for their quality and proven reliability.

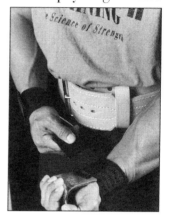

LIFTING HOOKS

During exercises like lat pulldowns, barbell shrugs and deadlifts the amount of time that you are able to keep going is often limited by the strength in your hands and fingers. This is unfortunate as those muscles are comparatively weak. Lifting hooks are a tremendous help in this area as they distribute the weight over your entire hand and wrist and enable you to continue to overload your larger muscles long after your grip would have let go. Highly recommended. Black $19.95

CRUNCH STRAP

Crunches are a great exercise for the abdominal muscles but they lack the ability to add intensity as the muscles get stronger. This limitation is overcome with the use of this clever device. The crunch strap is designed to attach to the low pulley of weight stack so that weight can be added to the exercise. Once the added intensity of weight is incorporated into this exercise your abs can develop to their maximum capability. Black- $19.95

LIFTING BELT

Nearly every exercise in Precision Training can be performed more safely with a good quality weight belt. Personally, I would never perform a standing barbell press, squat or deadlift without wearing a belt. The belt shown in this picture is custom made for us by a manufacturer who creates an excellent quality all purpose belt suitable for all but the most advanced lifters. Large 6" width and hook and loop fastener, very comfortable and requires no "breaking-in." Black. S-M-L-XL $29.95

GLOVES/WRIST WRAPS

These are the best lifting gloves in the world. Period. These gloves are made by the Harbinger company and have TechGel inserted into panels inside the glove for extra comfort and grip enhancement. They also have CoolMax lining to keep your hand cool, dry and comfortable by transporting moisture away from the skin. But best of all they incorporate a patented leather wrist wrap that securely supports your wrist during exercises like standing barbell presses, bench presses barbell curls and others. We've tries scores of gloves over the years and these ones are the only way to go. Black S-M-L-XL $29.95

T-SHIRTS/SWEATSHIRTS

Black ink on white cotton T shirt (pictured on the cover of the manual) or red ink on gray cotton fleece sweatshirt. Let them know you are using your head! Precision Training says you know what you are doing. M-L-XL T-shirts $16.95, Sweatshirts $24.95

LOG BOOKS

Replacement log books are available separately from Power Factor Publishing for $19.95

ORDER FORM

QTY	ITEM	PRICE	SIZE	TOTAL
	Lifting Hooks	$19.95		
	Crunch Straps	$19.95		
	Lifting Belt	$29.95	S-M-L-XL	
	Gloves/Wrist Wraps	$29.95	S-M-L-XL	
	T-shirts (Black on White)	$16.95	S-M-L-XL	
	Sweatshirt (Red on Gray)	$24.95	S-M-L-XL	
	Extra Log Books	$19.95		
	Shipping and Handling			$4.95
	Idaho residents add 5% sales tax			
	Foreign Orders (except Canada) add $10.00			
	All orders in US funds only.			

Send to Power Factor Publishing Inc.
10400 Overland Road, Suite #383 ■ Boise, Idaho 83709
Visa and Mastercard customers can call 1-800-376-6117 24 Hrs.